FBI & ATF Crimes, Lies and Cover-Ups

As exposed by Robert Rubino The Godfather of Christopher Wray, Director of the FBI

By Robert Rubino

Published by Native Book Publishing.

Genre: Non-Fiction, Crime, Criminal Law, Civil Rights

ISBN:

Printed in the United States of America

1st Edition

Table of Contents

Preface

I am about to take you on a disturbing journey. This book is not suitable reading for young people.

With malice of forethought, the FBI falsely and unscrupulously had me convicted of crimes they knew I did not commit to silence me for 20 incarcerated years about a humiliating FBI secret they were determined to conceal from the public. This text will reveal, through seemingly disjointed documents and pieces of information, the corruption, lies, and constitutional violations rampant in the FBI which belie the common belief in our constitutional rights: rights supposedly guaranteed to each of us in "We the People."

As you will see in the provided legal documents and associated evidence, I was, over the course of 18 terrible years, consistently denied access to courts and had my valid legal petitions rejected merely because these petitions were filed "too late" to be considered and were "time-barred" from being considered or adjudicated.

How can truth and justice be "too legally late" to be considered in the United States? I feel certain that this reality of our country—that, in the United States of America, such complete and brazen denials of our rights to fair trial and just treatment by our legal systems are not only possible but actively occurring—will come as a shock for most of you.

The disgraceful truth the FBI attempted to conceal through my false and malicious prosecution, in brief, is that **FBI special agent Robert Housholder** was in a then-illicit homosexual relationship with **three-time convicted child molester James Eckenrode** and that they further lived with and continually exploited a 16-year-old child for sex.

The FBI was not going to permit the public to learn the humiliating and criminal truth that one of their own was not merely gay but also a habitual child molester. Thus these criminals-with-badges spent years obstructing justice and using underhanded legal schemes to prevent the truth about Housholder and about my innocence from seeing the light of day.

I believe that it is my right and moral duty to now expose this underbelly of the FBI and the American judicial system. In the following pages, I intend to state everything I know about the crimes these criminals-with-badges committed in their pursuit of my unjust conviction and silence. I dare them to sue me in public or shut up.

Robert M. Rubino

Note from the Editor

This manuscript contains myriad references and quotations from legal documents which have been shortened and clarified for ease of reading. The full, unedited versions of these documents are included in this book's Appendix A in their original form. Furthermore, Appendix B includes several other legal documents for reference. Appendix C contains Mr. Rubino's full account of the medical issues he experienced while in prison and his reasoning for pursuing lawsuits against several related entities. Appendix D contains a more recent testimony by Mr. Rubino about the medical miracles he believes he has experienced, which he attributes to divine providence.

Introduction

My dear reader, the following narrative is a brief history of my 21+ years in prison for crimes I am not merely not legally guilty of committing but which I am totally innocent of any guilt or any involvement therewith but was maliciously framed for.

1) Federal FBI Special Agent Robert Housholder gave perjured testimony at my trial to falsely convict me in retaliation against me because I had provided proof of his being an active gay child molester living with his lover, a three-time convicted child molester he protected by making him an FBI Confidential Informant. This CI, James Echenrode, and Housholder had a 15 year old male prostitute also living with them named Raymond S.

As time passed and my complaints about their perversions could no longer be concealed, Echenrode's parole was suddenly violated, and, mysteriously, he died in prison only weeks after his incarceration. I believe his death was to prevent him from making a deal for his release in return for his testimony against Housholder, which would also have embarrassed the FBI totally.

2) My public defender, Trial Attorney Richard Layon, withheld the proof we now have that I had no knowledge of or involvement with the showing of a photo of a semi-nude adult woman to two boys. On October 31, 2024, I received a letter from the State Bar in which they enclosed an Attorney Misconduct Complaint Form to file against my trial attorney, Richard Layon. The Bar informed me that, "Your Letter Concerning a California Attorney." I did not send the letter referenced dated 10/24/24.

3) At my trial, the California State Laboratory Expert testified under oath that 5 sperm cells of mine and 6 cells with DNA from another unknown male were found in a spot the size of a nickel in the front of the alleged victim's boxers. In fact, this microscopic amount of specimen did not meet the minimum standard of admissible evidence under *People v. Kelly* (1976) 17 Cal. 3d 24; and *Frye v, United States* (D.C.Cir.1923) 293 F. 1013. This microscopic amount of alleged evidence was only found, the State Laboratory Expert testified, because San Diego Detective Victoria Reden told this lab tech where it was located and where it would be found. Only because she planted this false DNA and sperm evidence did she know where it was to be found! Reden planted this evidence to help FBI Special Agent Housholder falsely convict me and be able to imprison me to shut me up. Reden believed that, in return for

planting this false evidence for Housholder, he would help her become an FBI Agent!! I was and am innocent.

These criminals should be prosecuted under RICO for their crimes against not just me but against the very foundation of our state and U.S. constitutions. Their crimes constitute a permanent stain upon the integrity of our legal foundation of "**Justice for All**!"

Have a Blessed Day,
Robert M. Rubino

Chapter I

Statements of Pro Se Representation and Felony Obstruction of Justice and Brady Violations by FBI Director Christopher Wray and Superior Court Judge Runston G. Maino

The following documents and statements will demonstrate that FBI Director Christopher Wray, FBI Special Agent Robert Housholder, two California Superior Court justices, six San Diego district attorneys, a public defender, and other corrupt officials have committed serious crimes, including Brady violations, felony obstruction of justice, and perjury.

I will note that Christopher Wray has never once said I was guilty of anything and that he has also never said that FBI Agent Housholder is not a child molester. He also made no statement to defend Housholder's behavior because to do so he would have to lie.

These complex crimes demand, in the interest of justice, that our President order his Attorney General to initiate a Federal Criminal Conspiracy Grand Jury RICO Investigation!

A. On 10/11/12, Judge Brad Weinreb ordered the Office of the Public Defender to select a public defender to represent me. As of this date (4/2/24), I have had no response nor communication nor have I ever been informed of the name of the attorney who is supposed to represent me. I have not received any legal assistance that I am aware of. In addition, this Court denied my request to have Richard Crane, CDCR No. C-44519, represent me and prevented our direct communication. Therefore I must elect to represent myself, pro se, and proceed legally despite my lack of legal knowledge and inexperience with court procedures. I pray that this Court will extend me some latitude in this matter.

I am 81 years old (DOB 6/25/41) with numerous serious medical problems. I would prefer to attempt my representation before I die unjustly in prison.

B. On or about 2/15/07, Judge Maino sentenced me to 225 years in prison for my convictions. This was an unlawful sentence. Approximately one week later, I was recalled to the Court and Maino and prosecutor Clay Biddle both profusely claimed that the other was responsible for the unlawful sentence. My conflict attorney Layon, throughout all these sentencing procedures, said nothing to help me.

Next, Maino, in the presence of Biddle and Layon, for a second time unlawfully sentenced me, this time to 73 years plus life in prison. Maino used new sentencing laws which had been enacted only a few months earlier and were not applicable to alleged crimes which occurred before that 2006 enacted date. All three people present—Maino, Biddle, and Layon—must have known that my alleged 2003 crimes were supposed to be sentenced under the sentencing laws in effect in 2003 and that I could not legally be sentenced under these new 2006 laws.

Layon's dereliction of his duties as a conflict attorney are made particularly apparent by the Appellate Court's statement that, "if the Defendant's attorney had done his job properly, evidence of the Defendant's innocence would have been presented to the jury." Layon's silence during these unlawful sentencing procedures is further proof of the blatant refusal of anyone involved in my case to give me my due legal protections as a defendant. To demonstrate to the Court that this unlawful resentencing was both intentional and malicious I state the following facts:

On 11/4/21, I filed a 1054.9 petition which the Court granted on 3/22/22 (although to date I have never received a copy of that court order in spite of my several written requests to receive that court order copy). I once again formally request to see a copy of the 1054.9 court order.

The 11/4/21 1054.9 petition was received by Judge Maino, who at the time was still the acting superior court judge for my case. In this petition, I clearly and fully state that the sentence he imposed on me was unlawful and the reason why this was the case. I also wrote that I must be resentenced under the law in effect in 2003, when my alleged crimes were supposed to have occurred, and must be relieved of the sentence I was given under the 2006 sentencing laws which gave me an unlawful life sentence and an excessive term in prison. Despite this, Maino, with full knowledge that his sentencing had been illegal, did not correct his unlawful sentence.

By my estimate of the sentence permitted under 2003 sentencing laws, I estimate that I should have been sentenced to serve about 15 years, with no life sentence, with an allowance for time off for good behavior.

During the 20+ years I have served a prison sentence, I have never once been written up for a disciplinary violation. I pray that the Court will lawfully resentence me, taking into consideration the facts presented in my 1054.9 petition if possible. I also pray that the Court will order the State to compensate me financially for the actual and punitive damages and suffering I have endured for each and every additional day of incarceration I have served under the malicious and unlawful sentence. I do request the return of all fines, fees, and restitutions I have paid with appropriate interest. I do not consider myself a prisoner; I consider myself a hostage of the corrupt Judge Maino.

Furthermore, my 1054.9 petition cited numerous serious Brady violations committed by Maino. At the time when I was filing this petition, Maino was still my superior court acting judge and had ample opportunity to correct his unlawful sentencing. Maino chose to allow this and other Brady violations to remain in effect despite the fact that they were clearly exposed to him through the 1054.9 petition. Even a second-year law student would recognize that these violations must be corrected! I request that this Honorable Court refer these violations by Maino contained within these motions and in the 1054.9 petition to the Disciplinary Committee of the California Bar or other appropriate regulatory body for review.

C. It is my intention in this section C to cite to the Court what I believe constitutes only two of the violations described in the aforementioned 1054.9 petition. I request that the Court take judicial notice of all the Brady violations detailed in this petition, granted by the Court on 3/22/22.

For 20 years, the FBI withheld critical evidence, namely Tapes 39 and 40, from the Court. These tapes contained information favorable to the Defense, and the FBI's concealment of this evidence constitutes obstruction of justice and a very real felony offense. This intentional concealment of evidence was critical for then FBI Agent Housholder's perjured testimony at Rubino's trial and subsequent false conviction and resulted in the Defendant's losing his foster care license and being unjustly and falsely convicted of intending to transport children for sexual purposes. It is my belief that, were this evidence made available to the Court and to the jury, the outcome of Rubino's trial would have been changed and his verdict changed at least in part to Not Guilty.

In the past year, the San Diego District Attorney has confirmed to Rubino that the People recently recovered possession of Tapes 39 and 40 from the FBI and that the DA will copy these tapes and provide this discovery to Rubino in compliance with the Court's 1054.9 order. However, as of this date the San Diego DA has not provided these tapes and all of the discoveries granted by the Court under its 1054.9 order.

Please take note of Defendant's Motion to Strike People's Amended Response to Defendant's Request #15 Pursued to Penal Code Section 1054.9 dated 6/28/22, which demonstrates that the People have also obstructed justice by violating without just cause this Court's order to produce discovery. Please also note that Defendant's Reply to People's Opposition to Defendant's Application Pursuant to Penal Code 1054.9 dated 7/13/2022 details my above accusation with even greater specificity.

These two above motions state the facts that Superior Court Judge Henry Elias, for unknown reasons, was removed as judge and that Maino was selected to replace him in secret and that the Prosecution disregarded their U.S.-Supreme-Court-mandated constitutional duty, as established in *United States v. Bagley*, to disclose all material and information in their possession favorable to the Defendant. In violation of the U.S. Supreme Court decision, Maino ordered that the jury must not know anything regarding Iain R.'s serial sex assaults upon eight boys ages three to eight or Iain R.'s sodomy of a six-year-old victim's puppy with a stick. Further, Iain was not asked if he had had sex with nine year old T.J., a child involved in the case, because Judge Elias stopped Iain's confession under oath, stating to Biddle that the jury would "hate

[Iain]."

Maino's jury instruction was tailored toward producing his desired outcome for the trial and stated that "if [the jury] believe[d] the victim more than the Defendant, even in the absence of overwhelming evidence, [they could] find the Defendant guilty." Maino made no mention of the standard instruction that the jury must find the Defendant to be "guilty without a reasonable doubt" in order to be able to reach such a decision. Maino's jury instruction violates the Fifth, Sixth, and 14th Amendments to the U.S. Constitution. See *In re Winshep* (1970) 397 U.S. 358, 364; *Patterson V. New York* (1977) 432 U.S. 197, 210; *Sandstrom V. Montana* (1979) 442 U.S. 510, 513; *People V. Flood* (1998) 18C 4th 470, 482; see also *People V. Reyes Martinez* (1993) 14 CA 4th 1412, 1417.

Please also note that, as a superior court judge himself, Maino does not have the authority to override decisions made by another superior court judge, meaning that Maino should not have been able to override Superior Court Judge Elias' decision that Iain's sex crimes must be put on the court record and made public knowledge. If the jury had been made aware of Iain's crimes, as well as the fact that Iain was not prosecuted for or charged with these crimes in return for providing a false testimony against Rubino, the jury would almost certainly have returned a Not Guilty verdict even in spite of Maino's improper jury instruction mentioned above, and thus Maino's overriding Judge Elias' order constitutes another serious Brady violation.

Compounding upon these obvious and illegal mishandlings of Rubino's case, T.J. stated, under oath, that, "it's alright to lie if you have permission." When pressed by my lawyer, Richard Thomas, to explain what he meant by this statement, T.J. answered, "If you have to, you can lie to make things go right."

In this case, as in all others, justice delayed is justice denied! I make this appeal because, in the words of Thomas Jefferson, "Our Cause Is Just."

I, Robert M. Rubino, declare under penalty of perjury that the foregoing is true and correct. Executed 3/22/2023.

Robert M. Rubino

Proof of Service By Mail

I, Robert M. Rubino, hereby declare that I am over the age of 18, and I am a party to the herein action requested of my Public Defender attorney Emily Ross-Weber Esq. My legal address RJ Donovan Prison E24-A-104 480 Alta Rd San Diego Ca 92179

On 6/20/23 I mailed the following request to my attorney Ross-Weber Esq by placing a copy of the request in separate envelopes addressed as follows:

Honorable Presiding Justice McConnell
Fourth Appellate District Division One
750 B Street Suite 300
San Diego Ca 92101-8196

Hon Attorney General of California
1300 I Street
PO Box 390
Sacramento Ca 94244

Honorable Supervising Judge
Brad A. Weinreb
Superior Court of Ca County
of San Diego
North County Division Dept 22
325 South Melrose Dr
Vista Ca 92086-6695

Ms Summer Stephan
District Attorney of
San Diego County
330 West Broadway
San Diego Ca 92081

Mr. Christopher Wray
Director of the FBI
935 Pennsylvania Ave NW
Washington DC 20535

Chapter 2

The Code of Judicial Silence in Action

The following written reports and documents will detail my efforts to expose former FBI Agent Housholder's past criminal acts and to have the illegal concealment of evidence and proceedings in my trial addressed and demonstrate that no proper actions were taken by anyone in our corrupt judicial system. It is my belief that the following evidence exposes what can be termed a "Judicial Code of Silence," which tacitly approves the misconduct conducted by judges and continues to protect Maino from the consequences of his corrupt and unlawful rulings in the Rubino case.

Aside from Maino's misconduct as detailed in Chapter 1, this code also protected the actions and inaction of Arraignment Judge Nathan Goldstein, Prosecutor Clay Biddle, Public Defender Attorney Emily Rose-Weber, and the FBI at large. Six months before presiding as an arraignment judge in the Rubino case, Nathan Goldstein was a prosecutor (*not a judge*) in the Bonnie Dumanis District Attorney's Office in San Diego. Goldstein was bought by the District Attorney as a puppet judge to conspire with the prosecution to create the false and unjustly incriminating perception of the Defendant as a dangerous man. At the time of my trial, my entire criminal history consisted of one seat belt warning and some New York City parking tickets—I had never even gotten a speeding ticket.

To augment this false perception of the defendant's nature, Prosecutor Clay Biddle falsely and knowingly charged the Defendant with two counts of sodomy while knowing with certainty that, prior to any initial charges being filed, all medical tests performed on both T.J. and Iain had returned no evidence of sodomy having occurred. This corrupt prosecutor then proceeded, two weeks before trial, to drop the sodomy charges and to substitute them with the accusation that the Defendant's penis had touched T.J.'s and Iain's buttocks, again without any medical or physical evidence to substantiate his claim.

How could such charges be proved beyond a reasonable doubt when all medical tests contradict these claims and there is no evidence that the alleged physical contact ever occurred? The answer is simple. Simply have the presiding judge instruct the jury that they can find the Defendant guilty in the absence of overwhelming evidence. Again, Judge Maino stated to the jury, **"If you believe the victim more than the Defendant, even in the absence of overwhelming evidence, you can find the Defendant guilty."**

Beyond that, the result of these improper and illegal proceedings was that I was sentenced with 73 years plus life in prison and assigned a bail of six million dollars, as ordered by Arraignment Judge Goldstein. In my research I have found not one single instance in the past 75 years in which any defendant with no prior criminal history being charged with non-violent crimes, as I was, ever received anything close to this bail amount.

I also pose the following question to my reader: If a person were *actually* guilty of the non-violent inappropriate touching I was charged with, do you believe that the **73 year plus life sentence** I received was an appropriate and just sentence when for *murder* it would be decades less? Isn't this absurd sentence proof that I am the victim of judicial and prosecutorial corruption as well as FBI retaliation for my complaint against Special Agent Robert Housholder (which resulted in his being fired)?

If only I could have been tried by a court in China or Russia, I would have been found innocent and been free!

Declaration of Robert M. Rubino in Support of Post-Conviction Discovery

I, Robert M. Rubino, declare as follows:

1. In 1993 the petitioner filed a complaint against FBI agent Robert Housholder with the FBI Office of Professional Responsibility alleging Robert Housholder was in a then-illicit homosexual relationship with James Eckenrode, a three-time convicted child molester who was also his FBI Confidential Informant. This would later result in Housholder being terminated from the FBI. In retaliation, Housholder instigated and implemented a false and malicious investigation of the petitioner.
2. The results of the complaint and investigation were never produced to the petitioner and have been suppressed by the FBI despite the petitioner's repeated requests to know the outcome of the investigation and the facts found regarding these allegations. This suppressed evidence would strongly impeach Housholder.
3. The FBI told the petitioner that they were "not saying that [his] accusations [were] unfounded" and that they were "continuing to investigate." Because the facts and details of Housholder's bad character and abuse of authority were not made available to the petitioner, the petitioner was denied the right to impeach this witness.
4. The petitioner learned from Walter L., his foster and later adopted son, that Eckenrode had raped him when he was 7 years old. The petitioner was beyond furious and attempted to get proof against Housholder and Eckenrode. Housholder's retaliation against these actions by the petitioner forced the petitioner to initiate, at his own expense, a hearing to help keep his foster care license. At this ALJ Hearing, the judge ruled that the petitioner was not guilty of any crime.
    a. The petitioner attempted to have two boys who had been victims of Housholder and Eckenrode come to California to testify against them. Unknown to him, these boys did not exist and were instead an undercover Orlando police officer Rockerfeller.
5. The FBI has two tapes (39 and 40) which contain exculpatory evidence for the petitioner in his case. These tapes contain proof that the petitioner did not want to engage in any illicit acts as alleged in the case against him. Further, these tapes prove that Housholder testified falsely during the trial and reveal the circumstances which resulted in his termination from the FBI, which would impeach him as a witness.

6. Housholder threatened one of the petitioner's (guardian ad litem) children, Russel F., with numerous charges to attempt to coerce Russel into lying about the petitioner in court. Russel refused to lie, and Volusia County Judge Johnson threw Housholder out of his courtroom and offered to recuse himself due to Housholder's improper influence.
7. In conclusion, Housholder committed criminal fraud against the ALJ court, trial court, and petitioner. With an obsession to prevent the truth about the petitioner from being known, he used the power of a federal officer to intimidate related individuals, negatively influence the court, and corrupt facts in order to falsely and maliciously convict the petitioner.

I, Robert M. Rubino, declare under the penalty of perjury that the foregoing is true and correct. Executed November 4, 2021.

Robert M. Rubino ***Robert M. Rubino***

U.S. Department of Justice

Federal Bureau of Investigation

Washington, D. C. 20535-0001

July 12, 2010

Mr. Robert M. Rubino
REG# F61501
CSATF/SP
P.O. Box 5242
Corcoran, California 93212

Dear Mr. Rubino:

Your letter was forwarded to the Initial Processing Unit (IPU), Internal Investigations Section (IIS), Inspection Division (INSD), Federal Bureau of Investigation (FBI), for review. The IIS/INSD is the FBI entity responsible for investigating allegations of serious misconduct or criminal activity on the part of FBI employees.

In your letter you alleged that former Special Agent Robert Housholder and other individuals knowingly withheld proof of your innocence of attempting to transport a minor to California for sexual purposes. You alleged that the FBI had approximately forty taped phone conversations regarding this matter, but only produced two of the tapes.

The purpose of this letter is to inform you that the IPU/INSD has reviewed your allegations and has determined that there is no evidence of misconduct on the part of any FBI employee inasmuch as Mr. Housholder is no longer an FBI employee. Therefore, no further action will be taken by this office. Your concerns may be better addressed through the judicial system.

Sincerely,

Sandra A. Bungo

Sandra A. Bungo
Unit Chief
Initial Processing Unit
Inspection Division

Mr. Wray to cover-up Housholder's past criminal acts against me while he was an active FBI Agent, the IIS/INSD falsely claims and imply that they and the FBI are only responsible to investigate current active FBI Agents and not past allegations of misconduct by Housholder because he was terminated and is not a current FBI employee. His past criminal acts against me do not concern the FBI.

NONSENSE!

Robert M. Rubino

Attorney Emily Rose-Weber
Deputy Public Defender
Suite 900 Duplicate Original
451 A Street
San Diego CA 92101

Attorney Rose-Weber,

During my trial, then preceding Judge Harry Elias, heard Iain R[redacted]'s sworn confession in a special hearing that Iain was a sexual serial predator who sexually assaulted 8 boys ages 3-8 years old plus he sodomized one victim's puppy with a stick as it howled. Judge Elias said to the Prosecutor "How can you bring Iain into my Courtroom?" "The jury will hate him." The Judge ordered Iain's confession to be on the Court record of the trial. This quote and order by Presiding Judge Eliias confirms and proves that in Judge Elias's words, his legal opinion, that this sworn confession by Iain devastated the foundation of the Prosecution's case. I thought the case was over. Prosecutor Biddle had to get rid of Judge Elias from the trial and did! Biddle somehow shopped around and found Judge Maino who agreed to emphatically overrule Judge Elias's order to make public, on the record, Iain's confession which the jury must get. One Superior Court Judge, Maino, does not have the authority to override another Superior Court Judge's order but Maino did just that! This Maino order that the jury must not hear anything about Iain's sworn sex confession that he was a serial sex predator and details. Also Iain was not charged as promised for his sex crimes in return for his testimony against me which is perjured. This order to conceal evidence of Iain's crimes violates my rights as ordered by the U.S. Supreme Court, that all evidence favorable to the Defense must be presented to the jury with no exception. The U.S. Constitution also makes similar guarantees to assure a fair trial.

To further violate my Constitutional and U.S. Supreme Court rights to a fair trial was Judge Maino's jury instruction, "If you believe the victim more than the Defendant, even in the absence of overwhelming evidence, you can find the Defendant guilty." This jury instruction is an unconstitutionally lower standard of guilt required for conviction in every criminal case. It is similar to having the preponderance of evidence standard, not guilt beyond a reasonable doubt standard in all criminal cases and required for a guilty conviction. Maino's order to the jury denied my right to be found guilty beyond a reasonable doubt that all criminal cases require for conviction - no exception. If the above do not constitute a serious

Brady violation and reversal of all my convictions, then our U.S. and State Constitution do not protect us from violations of our rights.

Besides all the other serious trial violations I've endured, the Brady violation alone is sufficient to reverse all my convictions and my case. My Habeus Corpus, granted 3.22.23 on the point, has been signed by you and Judges Weinreb. Will you or won't you now, finally, address this serious Brady violation at least? Please decide and inform me so I can also decide what I must do to save my life from my false convictions.

I declare under pain of perjury that the hereinabove is true and correct.

Dated 11/26/23

In God's Hands I Am
Robert M. Rubino F61501
RJD-E24-A-101L

RICHARD CRANE, No. C-44519
R.J. Donovan Correctional Fac.
480 Alta Road, A-3-123
San Diego, CA 92179

EMILY ROSE-WEBER, PUBLIC DEFENDER
ATTORNEY AT LAW
451 A Street, Suite 900
San Diego, CA 92101-3623

November 06, 2023

[Re: PEOPLE vs. ROBERT MICHAEL RUBINO, CASE No. SCN167044]

Dear Ms. Rose-Weber:

I am writing on behalf of my brother Robert M. Rubino; and as Amicus Curiae I pursued the PETITION FOR WRIT OF MANDATE PROHIBITION, OR OTHER APPROPRIATE RELIEF filed October 13, 2022, and POINTS AND AUTHORITIES IN SUPPORT, citing how I was the individual who had prepared and litigated Mr. Rubino's Penal Code § 1054.9, and filings to disqualify Judge Maino under CCP §170.6.

Due to Mr. Rubino's being victim of an attempted murder stabbing, and without counsel, I requested to be allowed to proceed on his behalf under *In re Harrell* (1970) 2 Cal.3d 675; and *Storseth v. Spellman* (9th Cir.1981) 654 F.2d 1349 (The court gave Storseth and attorney, which mooted the need for inmate assistance by friend; but, reversed denial of the denial of Storseth's right to correspond with inmate assistant. *Id.* pp. 1355-1356.)

Please! Petition to have Mr. Rubino's sentence vacated and reduced to time served, immediate to full relief on the *Brady* violations which are overwhelming after receiving the withheld discovery of alleged victim Iain R[redacted]'s admitted sex crimes of children and a puppy who died from his assault with a stick.

Mr. Rubino was sentenced to life in violation of Ex Post Facto law in accordance with *People v. Hiscox* (1st Dist.2006) 136 Cal.App.4th 253 [Overview: Defendant's ex post facto claim in child sexual abuse case was not forfeited by counsel's failure to object, and prosecution's use of general testimony that did not establish at trial that the offense occurred after the effective date of Pen.Code, §667.61, precluded sentencing under § 667.61.]; also *People v. Riskin* (5th Dist.2006) 143 Cal.App.4th 234 [Overview: Because One Strike Law,

Pen.Code, § 667.61, took effect exactly five-and-one-half months after the beginning of the time frame for defendant's forcible lewd act offense, imposition of a One Strike term on that count violated the Ex Post Facto clauses of the United States and California Constitution.].

Mr. Rubino has asked me to intervene as counsel, but the court will not allow that; and, I am sure you are able to help him win relief; but, Please! understand that Robert needs immediate relief before he passes on.

The Ninth Court Circuit has followed the rule of law in reversing Ex Post Facto sentences. See United States v. Thomsen (9th Cir. 2016) 830 F.3d 1049, 1071: ("To implicate ex post facto concerns, amendments to the Sentencing Guidelines must present 'a sufficient risk of increasing the measure of punishment attached to the covered crimes.'" United States v. Waters, 771 F.3d 679, 680 (9th Cir.2014) (quoting Peugh v. United States, U.S. ..., 133 S.Ct. 2072, 2082, 186 L.Ed.2d 84 (2013)."

Mr. Rubino was sentenced in violation of Ex Post Facto law, and because his offense (which were non-violent) if true, required a greatly lesser sentence; and he should have been released years ago. See, *People v. Valenti* (2nd Dist.2016) 243 Cal.App.4th 1140, 1150: ("We vacate the indeterminate sentences imposed for courts 2 and 12 and remand for resentencing without application of the "One Strike Law.")

I sent Ms. Michelle Rogers extensive case law arguments with these and other cases to reverse Mr. Rubino's sentence. I asked her to forward the client file, and I wrote many letters to Randy Mize, concerning these same issues. The Ex Post Facto sentence was raised in the P.C. § 1054.9, citing these cases along with U.S. Supreme Court authorities.

On November 27, 2022, I filed and served the enclosed PETITION FOR TEMPORARY RESTRAINING ORDER AND PRELIMINARY INJUNCTION under Penal Code §§ 1473, and 147; plus, filed for compassionate release based in part on the attempted (preventable) murder of Robert Rubino.

Please! Forthwith file a Petition for writ of habeas corpus based on Robert's illegal sentence, to have him released pending the further resolution of the P.C. § 1054.9 habeas *Brady* issues.

Thank you very much for your work and help; but Mr. Rubino is 92 years old and needs immediate relief on the sentence.

The illegal sentence was known for over a year now, and this is not fair to Mr. Rubino who should be entitled to expedited relief.

I could have done this in two days. That is why I am really on Robert Rubino's side in this request.

Thank you very much for your time and consideration.

Yours truly,

Richard J. Crane
Richard J. Crane

Note to the Reader:
In spite of these letters, Weinreb-appointed Public Defender Emily Rose-Weber ignored all the issues raised by Rubino and Crane and prevented the Defendant from being present at his own hearings (2/5/23 and 1/10/24) or even learning about what occurred at these hearings despite the fact that a defendant is always allowed to be present at his court hearings.

Chapter 3

Life-Threatening Medical Negligence in Prison

As alluded to by Richard Crane in the letter enclosed in the previous chapter, I was stabbed with intent to murder during my time in RJ Donovan Correctional Facility. This was not the first time my life had been directly and physically threatened in E Yard.

Because of these threats to my physical safety, I have been made to "roll it up," or go to Administration Segregation, or AD-Seg, two times now. AD-Seg is colloquially referred to as the "hole" and is filthy—porters who clean are not permitted to enter the "hole" because it is a high risk security area.

The last time I was sent into AD-Seg, I had been stabbed, and my wounds immediately became infected. Not wanting my current knee replacement surgery site or lower leg open wound to also become infected, I sent a three page letter to both my brilliant orthopedic surgeon, Dr. James Bates MD, and to the Associate Warden for Specialty Services, Mr. Allan May, each with a copy of the other letter, explaining why I should not, in my medical state, be sent to the "hole." In response to this, Dr. Bates called Mr. May and explicitly gave his medical order that I was not to be sent to AD-Seg.

Despite this medical warning, on November 30, 2023, some custody CDCR officers sent me to the "hole." My leg wound became infected immediately, and, on December 5, 2023, I was rushed over 100 miles away to Centinela Prison's 15-bed intensive care emergency ward where, in addition to full hospital staff, four outside MD wound care specialists had to be called in to consult on my unknown and antibiotic-resistant infection. As of January 24, 2024, and *eight weeks* of treatment in solitary confinement, these doctors have still not been able to identify this superbug infection, although I am hopeful that my condition is slowly improving.

Dr. Bates has since resigned from his position as Chief Orthopedic Surgeon at CDCR, citing CDCR's wanton and callous disregard for his medical authority and for the health, life, and safety of his patient.

Enclosed in this chapter are excerpts from a letter I wrote to the San Diego Health Department describing my medical situation in greater detail and reporting on this unidentified superbug. I further enclose relevant medical refusal documents, prepared by the CDCR, demonstrating that CDCR medical officials were not only *not* able to kill off the unknown AD-Seg superbug after 8 weeks of intensive treatment and referrals to outside consultants but that they intended to keep me in 23/7 solitary confinement without any of my property despite the fact that my treatment could be continued at RJ Donovan's medical clinic in a regular open prison cell.

Report on RJ Donovan's Medical Negligence and Resulting Superbug, Excerpted from Rubino's Letter to San Diego Health Department

About two years ago, I was stabbed and placed in the very filthy AD-Seg, Administration Segregation, also called the "hole." My open wounds immediately became badly infected because the "hole" is never cleaned, with porters who clean other parts of the building not being permitted to clean AD-Seg because it is a high risk security area.

On November 3, 2023, my left knee was surgically replaced at Alvarado Hospital by Orthopedic Chief Surgeon Dr. James Bates MD. The RJ Donovan Prison Medical Clinic did a fine job daily cleaning and bandaging the open draining leg wound, which was kept infection-free.

On or about November 15, 2023, I informed Dr. Bates and Associate Warden Mr. Allan May in separate three page letters that I may have to "roll it up," for my personal safety was at risk on E yard. In these letters, I explained how critically important it was that I not be sent to the "hole" with my open leg wound because the "hole" is so filthy. I also sent both letters to Dr. Hausen PhD.

Dr. Bates has since confirmed to me, through a telemed phone call, that he responded to this letter by calling Mr. May and specifically issuing a medical order that I was not to be sent to the "hole" and explaining his reasoning for this decision.

At that time, I was also working on a soon-to-be-published manuscript exposing, along with previously mentioned FBI cover-ups, criminal acts against me by San Diego officials. The CDCR naturally does not want this information published or exposed. I mailed the original proof document to my editor, but, as of today, it has not reached him. This valuable original document was stolen from the RJ Donovan mailroom, and no one will address this.

That same day, I was sent to the "hole," where I immediately got the antibiotic resistant open wound bacterial infection. The timing of these two events is no mere coincidence. Along with theft of the U.S. mail, which is a federal crime, this constitutes yet another crime committed against me by CDCR staff, as forcing me into the filthy AD-Seg is at minimum felony elder abuse, if not attempted murder. Dr. James Bates' subsequent resignation from his position as CDCR's Chief State Orthopedic Surgeon further highlights the unacceptable and criminal nature of the CDCR's wanton disregard for my health, life, and safety.

I was sent to Centinela Prison Intensive Care on December 5, 2023. *Now seven weeks later*, January 24, 2024, they still cannot identify or cure this infection. In their efforts to identify this infection, the Centinela Infirmary has called in two outside MD wound care and one outside PA wound care specialist to consult without success. Am I a risk to the San Diego population with this antibiotic resistant bacterial infection?

The RJD "hole" and every other CDCR "hole" should be inspected and closed down as each of them is just as filthy and dangerous to the health of all staff and inmates as the last. I am 82 years old and prepared to meet my Lord and God. I am morally and civically obligated to inform you of the above even if it means my emotional stress and isolation.

Four other times the RJD has almost killed me through their neglect and medical incompetence. In one such event, misdiagnosed pneumonia sent me, almost dead, to the Scripps Hospital Trauma ER and then to the Alvarado Hospital Isolation ICU for eleven days. I could not be released from Alvarado until the San Diego Health Department cleared me! Here we go again?

Congratulations, CDCR and RJD: You have created in your AD-Seg a superbug even the military would be proud to have in its germ warfare arsenal!

STATE OF CALIFORNIA
REFUSAL OF EXAMINATION AND/OR TREATMENT
CDCR 7225 (Rev. 03/19)

DEPARTMENT OF CORRECTIONS AND REHABILITATION

CTC ORIGINAL

REFUSAL OF EXAMINATION AND / OR TREATMENT

PATIENT NAME (TYPE OR PRINT CLEARLY)	CDCR NUMBER	INSTITUTION
Rubino, Robert	F61501	CEN

Having been fully informed of the risks and possible consequences involved in refusal of the examination and/or treatment in the manner and time prescribed for me, I nevertheless refuse to accept such examination and/or treatment. I agree to hold the Department of Corrections and Rehabilitation, the staff of the medical department and the institution free of any responsibility for injury or complications that may result from my refusal of this examination and/or treatment, specifically:

Describe the examination and/or treatment refused as well as the risks and benefit of the intervention:

Refused admit to OHU. Informed of increase decline in health and possible wound complications. Patient aware of risks up to and including death. I refuse to continue to be held in solitary confinement 23/7 perday without property or tablet any longer

PATIENT SIGNATURE	DATE		DATE
Robert M. Rubino	1/25/24	☐ PATIENT REFUSES TO SIGN	

WITNESS

NAME OF WITNESS (PRINT/TYPE)		NAME OF WITNESS (PRINT/TYPE)	
I. De Leon RO			
WITNESS SIGNATURE	**DATE**	**WITNESS SIGNATURE**	**DATE**
[signature]	1-25-24		

1. Disability Code:
- ☐ TABE score ≤ 4.0
- ☐ DPH ☐ DPV ☐ LD
- ☐ DPS ☐ DNH
- ☐ DDP
- ☐ Not Applicable

2. Accommodation:
- ☑ Additional time
- ☐ Equipment ☐ SLI
- ☐ Louder ☐ Slower
- ☑ Basic ☐ Transcribe
- ☐ Other*

3. Effective Communication:
- ☑ Patient asked questions
- ☑ Patient summed information
- Please check one:
- ☐ Not reached* ☑ Reached
- *See chrono/notes

4. Comments: TABE 09.4

CDCR #: F61501
Last Name: Rubino
First Name: Robert
MI:
DOB: 06/25/41

Unauthorized collection, creation, use, disclosure, modification or destruction of personally identifiable information and/or protected health information may subject individuals to civil liability under applicable federal and state law.

Chapter 4

A Declaration of My Innocence

The following is a copy of a declaration I wrote so that my family and friends could point by point better understand my innocence.

1. When Russell F., a former ward of mine, was arrested in Florida for pot sales by FBI Special Agent Housholder, Housholder threatened him with ten years in prison unless he would tell lies about me as his former guardian. When Housholder went to Volusia County Judge Johnson to get Russ a long prison sentence because he refused to tell lies about me, Honorable Judge Johnson saw through Housholder's scam and threw Housholder out of his court. Judge Johnson offered to recuse himself as judge, but Russ agreed to serve a two-year prison term for pot sales. During this term, Russell's wife Pam and precious baby girl lived in my apartment with me and my two foster sons, Paul and Mike H. If anything improper were going on, Pam would surely have known about it!
2. We lived in Florida for one year, but it was too muggy and buggy! Around this time, the parents of Joey W., a friend of Russell F. and my ward Jason, were facing jail time for negligent parenting for Joey's being chronically truant from school. Joey's parents asked me if I could help because of all the legal experience I had accumulated as a result of being a foster parent for troubled young boys.

   In summary, the Florida Family Court Judge, after reviewing my history as a foster parent or guardian ad litem, confirmed and ordered that I become Joey's guardian ad litem. We then all moved to California except 19-year-old Russell who remained in Florida with his soon-to-become wife, Pam.

   In California, I registered Joey in school and explained his truancy problem. As a result, he received a psychological evaluation which found that he experienced panic attacks when sent to school. The psychologist described it as "throwing Joey into a snake pit." I asked to be referred to a child psychiatrist to treat Joey *at my expense*! Every week, Joey met for one hour with the MD psychiatrist who prescribed dilantin for him, and, once a month, the psychiatrist met with me and Joey together.

   Do you think I would provide this weekly care for one year and then continued medical care once a month thereafter if I were doing anything improper? I had two additional boys in my care at the time. Be certain that this MD asked every possible question about all of us and our home life.

After about 18 months, Joey's panic attacks stopped, and he was returned to his parents' custody in Florida.

3. Now I will relate the "short version" of a long, involved story. In 1991, I had been a foster parent for over 20 years; in fact, Wally, my adopted son, was married with one child and another on the way, my precious Danielle and Brooke. That year, I purchased the famous home of Jim and Tammy Bakker for $685,000—all 10,000 sq. feet of this home from the bankruptcy court.

About 18 months after I bought this house, an electrical fire burned down the house entirely. Living with me at the time were 16 people: friends who worked for me in my successful wholesale pizza business, Russell F. and his mother, and three boys I was guardian ad litem for at the time. The boys were 14 to 15 years old. The South Carolina State Arson Team, after a very extensive and public investigation, declared on TV that the fire was not arson but an electrical fire of "unknown origin." Please understand that if your home, for example, had a faulty electrical switch on the second floor of your home which causes your house to burn to the ground, the fire is determined to be of "unknown origin" because there is no longer any second floor to examine the faulty switch area. Nonetheless, arson specialists have so many ways to test for arson that investigation results declaring that the cause of a fire was not arson are certain. In fact, the South Carolina Arson Team believed that they knew the source of the electrical fire: I had, a week prior to the fire, replaced a larger floor standing AC unit, and a wall electric panel next to it was sparking and "arcing." This knowledge would later drive them to testify for me against my insurance company in court.

My insurance company was State Farm, and, unknown to me, State Farm trained agents for the FBI and ATF—for free!—in Quantico, VA. And, surprise! Three months after the fire, when the entire house debris had been cleaned up, ATF showed up at the request of their pals at State Farm and began a Federal Criminal Grand Jury investigation of the fire, of me personally, of my businesses and business history, and my 20+ years as a foster parent! I also got a huge IRS audit of my past (which actually resulted in my receiving a $23,000 tax refund check from the IRS because my accountants, per my instructions, were too conservative).

Usually, in a Federal Criminal Grand Jury investigation (I am told), you are found guilty of something 50% of the time within six months. If one year passes, that rate jumps to 90%. My investigation went on for *17 months*. Everyone around me was brought in to testify and be questioned by ATF and the Federal Prosecutor in the Grand Jury, including my four boys, Russell, David, Kenny, and Michael. They were asked about every aspect of my guardianship as well as about the house fire. The lead ATF agent (a lawyer) told my lawyer, Stonewall Jackson Kimball Esq., that "these boys are not smart enough to conceal anything illegal or improper from us finding out," and that they "[thought] of [me] as their father." Believe me, with the State Farm and ATF investigation going back years of my life, if there were anything bad for them to find, they would have found it.

16 months into the Federal Grand Jury horror and inquisition, Jack Kimball Esq. said he wanted me to hire a just-resigned U.S. Federal Prosecutor, whom U.S. Senator Strom Thurmond of South Carolina had nominated to become a federal judge. Then, Strom was called "the Lion of the U.S. Senate" and was very powerful politically. I paid one thousand dollars to these lawyers to advise me about the ATF Grand Jury investigation. Mr. Kimball Esq. wanted the Federal Prosecutor to see that I had VIP representation.

A few days after I met with this attorney, Mr. Kimball said that we had to go back to see the lawyers again because there was a problem. I was very concerned. What could be wrong? The attorney explained that the temporary law firm he was working for until his nomination to become a Federal Judge was confirmed had, years ago, once represented State Farm in a legal matter. Believing that this was a conflicting interest, the attorney believed that he could not represent me and intended to reimburse me the legal fee I had paid him. I immediately said, "Absolutely not; that is your money and I will not take it back because of some legal nonsense. I will sign a waver or whatever, but that is not my money. I hired you to advise me, and you did. The money doesn't belong to me."

At that point, things were tight for me financially, and I vividly remember the event. Jack Kimball Esq. smiled and said, "I told you Mr. Rubino is an honest man." The attorney smiled and gave me a handshake.

Then unknown to me, this attorney went and spoke to Senator Thurmond (his mentor for years) and told the Senator all about me, including about my being a foster parent. He told Thurmond all about the ATF-State Farm quid pro quo federal investigation against me, as well as about the fire and everything else. Upon hearing this, the Senator, in the attorney's presence, got on the phone with the head of ATF—the same man who ran ATF during the Waco Massacre—and said, as he later related to Jack Kendall and then me, in his southern drawl, "I understand you are investigating a constituent of mine, a Bob Rubino. He's the fellow who bought Jim Bakker's house. I understand that my South Carolina State Arson boys thoroughly investigated the fire and said it is clean, but your friends at State Farm got you to begin a now 17-month-long Grand Jury Criminal Investigation of this honest man. I would like you to keep me informed and advised of this investigation."

Well, the head of ATF called his head ATF agent and said, "Put the Hammer down," which means uncock the gun. The ATF agent called Jack's office and said, "The Grand Jury Investigation is over. Your client is clean." I sued State Farm and was jury awarded $715,000 actual; $850,000 punitive; $110,000 interest; and $453,000 legal fees, and I sold the land for $100,000 more.

Do you realize how clean every aspect of my life had to be for me not to be charged or convicted of even a jaywalking ticket? Mr. Kimball, later Judge Kimball Esq., said he knew of no one else who could survive such an extensive inquisition as I did. He said that I was questioned by all of them 83 times, and they never once caught me in a lie! As I said to him, **you don't have to be smart to tell the truth**. In spite of ATF and State Farm investigators going back years and speaking to former foster sons and anyone else they thought could reveal something negative about me, and despite the Bakker house fire not only making national news but international news as well, they could find nothing because, during the first 62 years of my life, my entire criminal history consisted of one seat belt warning and some NYC parking tickets.

If anyone has any questions about me or about my character, let them ask themselves if they could have survived the above detailed Federal Criminal Grand Jury-ATF investigation.

I declare under penalty of perjury that the above is true and correct.

Dated 3/29/23

Respectfully yours,
Robert M. Rubino

Chapter 5

Who I Am

It is my hope that, by sharing with you the lives of my "hard to place" boys, you will come to understand why I live the words of my Savior Jesus Christ, "Suffer the little children come unto me" (Mark 10:14).

The following two young lives—as unique and tragic as they were medically, emotionally, and socially—were quite typical of the diverse care I had to learn to provide for the specialized needs of each boy under my care.

In every case, my unconditional acceptance for each child and my unconditional love for them as their father had a profound and miraculous healing effect on them in contrast to their past lives of emotional and physical deprivation. It is still a joy to me to have witnessed the wonderful new life born into each one of my sons.

Billy

When I was living in Florida, Joey W. began for the most part to live with me, Jason, and Russell in our 3-bedroom apartment. Joey was dating Karen B., whose parents were divorcing and who had a younger brother named Billy.

Billy had a badly deformed mouth and jaw and was a psychologically diagnosed "failure to thrive" child. His mother's new boyfriend refused to have Billy move with her and Karen to their new home in Pennsylvania, and Billy's father also refused to take custody of him because he was a very angry and difficult child. Billy would fight anyone who bothered him, no matter how much physical damage he himself would take. He also always kept one hand over his mouth to hide his facial deformity, especially while eating.

Surprise—Billy just became one of us! Each morning when I woke up and came into the living room, Billy was sleeping on our couch. Billy felt my acceptance of him. I called him my marmot. He had a terrific sense of humor.

Then, Billy broke into a Florida State Trooper's house and stole his gun and some electronics and was caught. In Juvenile Hall, Billy was so antagonistic toward a worker that this person kicked Billy in his groin and caused him to be taken to the hospital. Because his mother demanded that this worker be changed and threatened to sue, they released Billy back to her. I was moving to California at the time, and Billy's mother begged me to take custody of Billy "temporarily." I agreed, not knowing that he was a fugitive.

In California, an oral surgeon donated his skills to extensively reconstruct Billy's disfigurements. Then I got braces for Billy, which he needed and cost me $6000 over the next two years. During this period, Billy grew from 4'11" to 5'9" and from 68 pounds to 138 pounds—his psychological "failure to thrive" diagnosis no longer existed!

Every six months, I sent Billy to visit his family in Pennsylvania. During the last few visits, he met a girl he later married. When his braces finally came off, he had a handsome face and smile. He got a retainer to wear at night, and I reunited him with his family in Pennsylvania.

Unfortunately, Florida learned he was in Pennsylvania and descended to extradite him back to Florida. I hired a Pennsylvania attorney to fight this extradition. When Florida learned of Billy's good behavior and school record over the past two years and, just as importantly, how much it would cost Florida to send an attorney to Pennsylvania, as well as of his mother's still possible lawsuit, they dismissed Billy's charges. My Marmot, my son, my little Billy, was free to begin his positive, wonderful life!

Vincent H. AKA Vincent R.

The Thursday before Easter of 1979, Vinnie H., a friend of my later-adopted son Wally, stayed overnight so the boys could go skateboarding early the next morning.

At about two in the morning, Vinnie came into my room and woke me up. He had a very painful earache. I took him into the kitchen and, with a basting tool and some warm water, flushed out his ear, which released quite a lot of discharge and gave Vinnie some relief. I told him to go home in the morning and have his mother take him to a doctor.

I did not know at the time that Vinnie was not simply a "hard to place" NYC Child Dependency Ward but a "throwaway." This NYC child agency no longer even bothered to look for him. I would later learn that Vinnie was nicknamed "Houdini" because he was an expert at bypassing store alarm systems, allowing his pals to then rob the store and to give him his share. Because he was only 15 and an NYC ward, not much would happen to him if he got caught.

Late afternoon on Easter Saturday, Vinnie came to my apartment and asked me if he could rest there because he had a sinus infection and had some pills he could take for this. His speech was slurred, his vision was somewhat blurred, and he stumbled as he tried to walk. With Wally's encouragement and after half an hour of pleading and promising to be there for him, Vinnie trusted Wally and me to take him to the Lenox Hill Hospital ER. I was known to them as a licensed foster parent from my many visits there over the years, and by 6 PM he was diagnosed to have a neglected ear infection that had now, most likely terminally, infected his brain.

Because they could not locate his mother, the hospital had to operate by the authority of an emergency court order, and Vinnie had little chance to survive the eight-hour operation. I was asked if I would stay with him until they put him to sleep, and, of course, I did. Before 6 AM on Easter Sunday, I was by Vinnie's bedside with an Easter basket.

With slurred speech, he said, "You're here to tell me goodbye," and tried to smile. He had never had an Easter basket before, from the "Easter Bunny" or anyone. I assured him that I would be waiting for him when he came out of recovery and that we'd eat up his Easter basket. The knowing, slight smile he gave me, I can't adequately convey to you, but it broke my heart that I was the only person in his life to be with him in what was possibly the last hour of his life!

Wally and I had been invited to have Easter dinner with friends of mine. I explained that I had to be in the hospital for Vinnie in case he survived the brain operation. Of course, they agreed, and we said a prayer for Vinnie together.

The operation was a success! Before Vinnie regained consciousness, his surgeon explained to me that he would be deaf in the removed inner ear, that he would be partially blind, and that he would have a dropped lip and foot and slurred speech, but that he was alive! He asked me if I could be a father figure to him, as he had no one, and a positive mental attitude could greatly improve his recovery chances. I told the surgeon that Vinnie had only agreed to come to the ER because I promised to be with him and that I keep my promises. I was going to be there for him.

When my Vinnie became conscious, we shared his Easter basket.

Vinnie was in Lenox Hill Hospital for over three months, and, every day, I was there for his lunchtime and dinnertime, often with his favorite things to eat to cheer him up. One day, on a dare, I made two pounds of spaghetti with my own meat sauce and fed the entire pediatric ward, to Vinnie's delight. Because he was on steroids, he ate a lot and went from 95 pounds to 121 pounds before he was released.

Twice, in frustration at his hospitalization, Vinnie acted up. The first time, he barricaded himself in his hospital room and refused to get another IV inserted. The hospital called me, and, upon my arrival, he calmed down because I promised, and the hospital staff had agreed, that he could simply shoot his meds that night. He and I kept count, and he had had 147 IVs collapse up to then. Another time, he barricaded himself in his room and was throwing things out his window onto the sidewalk and street three floors below. For this wild street child to be confined was frustrating. I was called, and my arrival and talk with him again calmed my little Vinnie down, and this incident passed.

Now, miraculously, Vinnie's vision returned 100%, and he had no drop lip or foot and was walking perfectly with no paralysis at all. He was deaf in the ear they had removed a part of to prevent water from going into his ear and brain. I found Vinnie a company that made him a custom device to put on his ear so that he could swim and keep water out of his ear when he was in the shower.

Vinnie had had a 2"x3" section of his skull removed and had only scalp covering his brain over that section. The surgeon had to wait six months to close his skull to be sure that the infection did not return. He would have grand mal seizures and be on phenobarbital, dilantin, and other meds always. Praise God for this recovery!

One day, I was called to the hospital where I was confronted by Vinnie's surgeon, head nurse, social worker, Catholic priest, and Episcopalion minister. How could I have not seen this coming? They had no place or person that Vinnie could stay at or with and be safe. Would I be his foster father? Vinnie only trusted me and Wally. His medical risks were great: one hit on his head would kill him. I told them, "God brought this child to me, and He has miraculously healed him. I know He will guide and provide for us." From that moment, Vinnie was legally my foster son.

Months before, the psychologist had told me that Vinnie was a true sociopath, telling me that "he could kill someone and sit down next to the body and eat lunch," that "he has no sense of guilt or remorse," that "he does not understand why you care about him or Wally," and that "he only sees that you do."

About four months after Vinnie was placed in my care, I received a call from 100 Center Street, where they do arraignments 24/7 and have a jail in the basement called "the Tombs." I've been there many times for my boys, and many of the judges know my name and reputation. As I walked down the aisle of this huge courtroom with a 20-foot-high ceiling, the judge humorously called out, "Here comes the cavalry," and everyone laughed and stared at me.

The judge called Vinnie, who was sitting in the Dock (he could not be held in the Tombs because of his medical vulnerability), stopped the ADA from reading his charges, and asked Vinnie why he had beat up some guy and how old each of them were. Vinnie answered that he was 15 and the kid 18, and that the other kid was a "punk" who had called his girlfriend a "bitch," and so he "beat his ass." The judge told Vinnie, "He could have killed you with one blow to your head," and Vinnie very seriously replied, "Who cares?" He had absolutely no sense of self-worth!

The judge said, "Mr. Rubino would miss you." Absolutely surprised by this, Vinnie turned to me and asked me, "You would?" He couldn't understand why I or anyone else would miss him. I replied, "Of course I would miss you. You are my son." The judge asked me if I would take him home, and I replied, "Of course." He waved off the ADA and declared the case dismissed for lack of evidence, then said to Vinnie, "Listen to your dad and be a good boy."

Six months after Vinnie's placement with me, his skull was closed and repaired. Legally, his mother had to sign him out of the hospital and take custody of him, and she did, bringing him out of the hospital with his head in a bandage. Just outside the hospital front door, she gave him a subway token, told him, "Stay with your uncle tonight and find another place by tomorrow," and left him. Of course, he came to me. For the next five months, until the Department of Social Services realized he was still with me, his mother collected welfare payments for him.

Later, the family court judge apologized to me for NYC not providing me foster payments. They could not reimburse me because Vinnie's mother was still being paid. The judge was angry at the social workers' failure to catch this and told the two of them present that I was an "NYC valuable asset" who took many of their placements no one else would accept. I smiled and told the judge, "I didn't care about the money. Vinnie was my son, and God had placed him in my care!"

Many years later, I received a call from the Lenox Hill Hospital Head Social Worker who had just spoken with Vinnie. He had earned his AA in Mortuary Sciences and prepared dead bodies for funerals: a job that required no emotions or feelings. She continued and said that my being in his life and my four years of caring for him saved some family from a tragedy. She told me that she had asked Vinnie, "What do you think of Mr. Rubino?" and he had replied, “He’s the only one who won’t hurt you. He’s the only one I never robbed.” All my sons; so many stories!

The greatest injustices were the additional children’s lives I could have saved during my 20-year false imprisonment. Haters exposed their lack of Christian character; because they wouldn’t selflessly help a child, they cannot believe that someone else will!

In God’s Hands, I am
Robert M. Rubino

10/9/23

"It is Done"[1]

Because I speak the truth
Their lies can't affect me.
Because God protects me
Their hate won't corrupt me.
Because I don't give up
My character sustains me.
They may try to kill me
But my innocence will out live me.
Their lives are a blasphemy
And eternal damnation their reality.
I forgive and pray that someday
They accept my Christianity!

By
Robert M. Rubino

[1] "It is Done" are the last words Jesus spoke from the cross before He died.

About the Author

Robert M. Rubino grew up Catholic in a close Italian family. He attended Princeton County Day School as a child and earned his high school diploma at Lawrenceville Prep School. After this, he was accepted to Georgetown University, where he earned a BA in English and minored in theology.

Eight days before he entered Georgetown, Rubino's nine-year-old brother, Johnny, died in his arms on the way to the hospital because of a sudden brain aneurysm. The experience of feeling Johnny go through the process of dying in his arms had a lifelong, profound effect on Rubino, who marks this tragedy as the moment when he learned the precious value of every child's life.

While at Georgetown, Rubino was a member of the Confraternity of Christian Doctrine (CCD), through which he taught Catechism and Confirmation classes to 3rd and 4th grade children who did not attend a Catholic school. Based on this experience, he was later asked to volunteer as a lay counselor at St. Joseph's Home for Boys for boys up to twelve years of age.

Just before Rubino's graduation from Georgetown, Rubino was asked to meet with the Honorable Chief Presiding Baltimore Juvenile Court Judge Robert I.H. Hammerman. Unknown to him, the Sister Superior of St. Joseph's had recommended him to Judge Hammerman to become involved in a new experiment testing the possibility that single people could one day become licensed foster parents. This experiment, conducted by seven judges across the nation, would, if successful, allow single people to also adopt and foster the countless thousands of children languishing in state institutions because of the dearth of couples willing to accept them. If Rubino accepted, he would essentially become a parole officer for a 14-year-old boy caught stealing a blanket off a clothesline at night so he would not freeze, and would have to assume all financial cost and responsibility for the boy's medical bills, education, clothing, and care. Rubino did indeed accept this arrangement, and the boy's placement was a terrific success that led to single people being allowed to become licensed foster parents just two short years later.

A few years after this first child was returned to his family, Judge Hammerman recommended Rubino for another childcare experiment, which sought to test whether a foster child could be placed outside of the neighborhood he had been living in (as, at the time, it was the norm to place a foster child back in their own neighborhood even if the neighborhood was unsafe). Thus, after a home and psychological evaluation by the District Attorney's office in NYC, Rubino became the first out-of-state licensed foster parent in the history of Pennsylvania.

Having found his passion and gift for raising "hard to place" boys, Rubino proceeded to become a **guardian ad litem** or licensed foster parent to **39 boys** with every type of medical, physical, emotional, and social problem, including five with AIDS. Over the thirty years in which he served as guardian for these children, there was not one negative report of the care he provided, and he received many letters of praise from professionals for his guardianship of these "hard to place" children.

At 82 years old, Rubino is determined to meet his God without anger, hate, or vengeance in his heart. He forgives everyone who was involved in his wrongful conviction and irresponsible medical treatment without mental reservation. He made a vow of celibacy when entering prison, which he has kept and plans to keep until his death.

The following pages contain letters pertaining to Rubino's innocence and attesting to Rubino's excellent work as guardian and foster parent and to his good character.

IN THE INTEREST OF : IN THE COURT OF COMMON PLEAS OF DAUPHIN COUNTY, PENNSYLVANIA

WALTER [redacted] : NO. 243 JUVENILE DIVISION 1977

ORDER OF COURT

AND NOW, this 13th day of March, 1978, after hearing in the above matter, the Court places the juvenile in the custody of Robert Rubino, 170 E. 78th St., New York, New York. It is ordered and directed that as custodian, Mr. Rubino shall have the right to the physical custody of the juvenile, the right to determine the nature of the care and treatment of the juvenile, including medical care, and the duty to provide for the care, protection, training and education of the juvenile.

It is further ordered and directed that the above-named juvenile shall not be released from the aforementioned custody without the express approval and Order of this Court.

BY THE COURT:

JUDGE

Distribution:
Clerk of Courts
Judge Richard B. Wickersham (2)
Probation Office
Robert Rubino
Public Defender's Office
County Controller
Kathleen McCabe

Certified: March 13, 1978
Clerk of the Court

BOARD OF EDUCATION OF THE CITY OF NEW YORK

HAAREN HIGH SCHOOL

899 TENTH AVENUE NEW YORK, N. Y. 10019

BERNARD V. DEUTCHMAN
PRINCIPAL

TELEPHONE
265-4150

June 15, 1978

To: Mr. Robert Rubino
Re: Walter [redacted]
Fr: Gregory Luszcz

Dear Mr. Rubino:

It pleases me greatly to inform you of the substantial progress Wally has made at Haaren H.S., this past semester. His attitude towards school has made a complete turnabout demonstrated by his increased interest in the academics, positive remarks from his subject class teachers and his conversations with my staff concerning his program for the fall semester. Due to his eagerness to work with the Reading Volunteers it has been reported to me that his reading level has increased considerably. Your continuing cooperation and concern for Wally's education is one of the most important ingredients for his success at Haaren H. S. If you have any questions concerning his program for the fall semester, please do not hesitate to call or visit the school.

Sincerely
Gregory Luszcz
Gregory Luszcz
Program Chairman

(29)

PROBATION AND PAROLE OFFICE

CRIMINAL DIVISION
Dauphin County Courthouse
Harrisburg, Pennsylvania 17101

JUDGE RICHARD B. WICKERSHAM
JUVENILE COURT JUDGE

JUVENILE DIVISION
17 South Second Street
2nd. Floor – Menaker Build
Harrisburg, Pennsylvania 17

WILLIS W. HOOVER
CHIEF PROBATION OFFICER
TELEPHONE 255-2680

December 18, 1978

Judge Robert I.H. Hammerman
Court House
Baltimore, Maryland 21202

Re: Walter [redacted]

Dear Judge Hammerman,

I am writing to you in behalf of Mr. Robert Rubino of 170 E. 78th Street, New York, New York. In February of this year you submitted a letter of recommendation to the court of Dauphin County in behalf of Mr. Rubino who was interested in becoming a foster parent to Walter [redacted] Since March of this year, Walter has been living with Mr. Rubino in New York. Since his placement with Mr. Rubino, Walter has made magnificent progress. Walter precently has a part time job and will soon begin tutoring for his GED. His relationship with Mr. Rubino has grown to be very close, one in which Walter views Mr. Rubino as his older brother. For once in his life, Walter has a real sense of security and self-worth. These positive feelings, I attribute to Mr. Rubino's overwhelming patience, courage, concern, understanding and basic love for a young man who was deeply troubled.

I personally want to thank you for your help in making this placement possible.

Sincerely,

Deborah A. Miller

Deborah A. Miller
Juvenile Probation Officer

DAM:jt

Supreme Bench
of
Baltimore City

ROBERT I. H. HAMMERMAN
JUDGE

COURT HOUSE
BALTIMORE, MARYLAND 21202

December 26, 1973

Mr. Robert M. Rubino
1105 Lexington Avenue
New York, New York 10021

Re: Walter [redacted]

Dear Mr. Rubino:

I have received your letter of December 20, 1973, as well as the Christmas card from you and Walter. I appreciate both.

Needless to say, I am very delighted at the progress which Walter has made and have been most pleased to have Walter stop in a couple of times on his own to see me. There seems to be evident to me a much more mature and a much happier young man.

I would be pleased to concur with your judgment and recommendation and will, at this time, terminate his probation to this Court. I am doing this through a copy of this letter to Mr. Edward J. Lang. I would appreciate the voluntary reports which you have suggested for no other reason than the fact that I will continue to be most interested in Walter and his welfare.

It is no exaggeration to say that almost all of the credit for Walter's substantial progress lies with you. Your interest and contribution has not only been singular, but amazing to say the least! I am confident that the rewards which are due you will be forthcoming.

My very best wishes to you and to Walter for the holiday season and for a wonderful and successful New Year.

Sincerely,

JUVENILE PROBATION OFFICE

17 SOUTH SECOND STREET • 2ND FLOOR MENAKER BUILDING • HARRISBURG, PENNSYLVANIA 17101

JUDGE JOHN C. DOWLING
JUVENILE COURT JUDGE

STEPHEN J. SUKNAIC
CHIEF JUVENILE PROBATION OFFIC
TELEPHONE 255-2680

September 18, 1980

Mr. Robert Rubino
170 East 78th Street
New York, New York 10021

Dear Mr. Rubino,

I was very happy to finally meet with you. I am glad to see Wally is doing fine wi your guidance. I would like to express my appreciation for all your efforts and concern which have nullified Wally's delinquent behavior. Through your guidance, you have shown Wally that it is possible to survive in this world without exhibiting negative behavior. Wally has now seen and felt what it is like to live a positive lifestyle; something whic could not have been possible without your help. Hopefully, Wally will now use the tools which you have given him to lead a positive and rewarding life.

I am happy to hear you are considering accepting another boy or two, for possible future foster placement. I personally feel that juveniles who have a terrible family situation, such as Wally, benefit immeasurably when placed in a positive living situatio such as you provide.

Regarding Wally's visit to the hospital, I have forwarded the bill for his medicine to our financial department. You can expect reimbursement in the near future.

I again thank you for the work you have done with Wally. Now that the time is drawing near for Wally to start out on his own, I am confident that you have given him the potential to lead a successful life. It must be rewarding to you. Take care and please contact me if I can be of any further assistance.

Sincerely,

Keith B. Snyder

Keith B. Snyder
Juvenile Probation Officer

BS:keb

WEST SIDE SCHOOL OF NEW YORK CITY
DAY TREATMENT CENTER
333 WEST 86 STREET, NEW YORK, N.Y. 10024 (212) 874-6200

May 2, 1983

Re: Brian [redacted] , DOB: 7-17-66
ADM: 3-16-81

To Whom It May Concern:

Brian [redacted] has been a student at the West Side School since 3/81 . During this period Brian has demonstrated a wide range of oppositional behavior as well as social strengths. Initially, Brian's presenting problem was rooted in a rageful and intense relationship with his mother mixed with emotional and learning complexities which emerged in school, home and the community. Brian was unable to relate to this worker and teachers without inappropriate and disruptive behavior. Brian's attendance was irratic and when in the classroom it was quite evident he was in need of space and time to settle down. Brian's success was not to be realized until he was somehow separated from Mother, however he would not accept another institutional experience. Brain had just come from Hawthorne Cedar Knolls which was experienced by him as an abandonment by his family.

Presently, Brian is living with Mr. Rubino with the consent of his Mother and at his own wish. This is the second time living with Mr. Rubino since 1981 and this present living arrangement seems much more stable as goals have been defined, as well as expectations established and rules followed. Brian's oppositional behavior has decreased significantly. He is more able to work in the classroom i.e. approach a task with less anxiety and follow it through to its completion. Attendance has been excellent and Brian is more willing to participate in informally arranged treatment sessions.

(con't on page 2)

(30)

WEST SIDE SCHOOL OF NEW YORK CITY
DAY TREATMENT CENTER

333 WEST 86 STREET, NEW YORK, N.Y. 10024 (212) 874-6200

MRS. K. EVAN FRIEDMAN, *Chairperson*
CHARLES H. KING, A.C.S.W., *Director*

Re: Brian [redacted] - con't 5/2/83
DOB: 7-17-66
ADM: 3-16-81

Perhaps Brian has come to realize this is his time to take on responsibility for his life. Whereas Brian was once isolated from fellow students, presently he is well liked, and a positive peer role model. Brian was elected president of the Student Council for 1983.

Sincerely,

Vincentine Loverro, CSW
Psychiatric Social Worker

VL/jw

(31)

DECLARATION

My name is Cheyenne [redacted]. I was born Aug. 7, 1994 which makes me sixteen years old. I met Mr. Rubino and his grand daughter Brook when I was in 3rd grade.

One day, when I went to Mr. Rubi o's apartment to play with his granddaughter Brook, I s w Iain [redacted] download a photograph of a nude woman from the internet onto Mr. Rubino's computer. The woman in the photo had dark hair and wore a bra and panties. When she took them off you could see her breasts and pubic area. Mr. Rubino was not in the room with us. He didn't know about the photograph or what Iain was doing. He didn't even know how to use the internet!

Later that day I went to the park behind Mr. Rubino's apartment and Iain was there. Iain was showing the same picture of the naked woman to TJ [redacted] and the kids playing there. Mr. Rubino wasn't in the park with us. He still didn't know about the photograph Iain had or what he was doing with it.

I was willingly going to testify in court about what I saw that day. But at the trial, Mr. Rubino's attorney <u>never questioned me about it.</u> So, I couldn't let the court know about Iain [redacted] downloading a photo of a nude woman from the internet onto Mr.Rubino's computer or what went on in the park later that day.

I declare under penalty of perjury that the foregoing statements are true and correct.

Signature *Cheyenne B.D* Feb.17,2011

Cheyenne [redacted]

Witness *Vita Banks* Feb.17,2011

Vita Banks

LAW OFFICES OF ALEXANDER C. VERDUCI
380 S. MELROSE DR., SUITE 207
VISTA, CALIFORNIA 92083

TELEPHONE (760) 643-4030
FACSIMILE (760) 643-4077

FILED
Clerk of the Superior Court
JUL 12 2002
BY: CHARI LYON

May 21, 2002

The Honorable Richard G. Cline
Superior Court of California, County of San Diego
North County Division, Probate
325 S. Melrose Dr
Vista, CA 92083

Re: STATEMENT OF ISSUES AND CONTENTIONS, MINORS' COUNSEL'S REPORT: CASE OF ***ALEXANDRIA*** [redacted] ***dob*** [redacted] case # PN 82523

INTRODUCTION

A. I was appointed as Minors' Counsel by order of The Honorable Richard G. Cline by his Order dated 5/29/02.

B. The primary issues presented at the time of appointment were appropriateness of appointing paternal grandfather of minor child as Guardian of the Person as requested in his Petition filed 11/26/2001

INFORMATION RECEIVED

1. Multiple Individual office and telephonic meetings were conducted with Petitioner and the minor client who was seen both separately and with Petitioner.

2. Documents were reviewed to include the entire Court file, the FCS Report and attachments.

1

35

3. Observations of the minor child interacting with Petitioner.

4. Detailed Psycho-Educational Report, Individual Summary of Assessment Report completed by the San Marcos Unified School District on the minor child was reviewed.

5. Letter from minor child's Psychiatrist, Monique Masse, M.D.

STATEMENT OF ISSUES AND CONTENTIONS

Petitioner Grandfather requests that the Temporary Guardianship currently in place be made permanent. The colorful, if not amazing history of Petitioner, under the circumstances suggest that a closer look concerning his fitness be made.

DISCUSSION

Petitioner has demonstrated a life of what appears to be selfless service to others, both family and non-family members. The questionable issues raised by Family Court Services seem to focus on judgment issues centered on Petitioner's zeal to serve and or rescue individuals in need. Nothing that I have reviewed or investigated have in any way suggested that Petitioner grandfather is or would in any way be unsuitable to continue to provide the nurturing care and support for Brooke that he has so lovingly been providing since her birth.

In fact, the evidence suggests that there is no one better suited or committed to provide for her care and special needs. It would be devastating to the child, particularly in view of the multiple tragedies in her life, to remove or in any way interfere with her relationship with her grandfather.

Additionally, I see no need for Petitioner to be subjected to an intrusive psycho-sexual evaluation in this case. There has never been any credible evidence to suggest that he has harmed children and there most certainly is no evidence that he has been anything but a savior to his granddaughter.

36

The difficulty with this case is that we have become too jaded in our society to accept the fact that good and selfless people can exist in our world and not be as heroic of a figure as Mother Theresa. Mr Rubino is a good man who loves his granddaughter and has dedicated his life to her at a time when she is most in need. I agree with the professionals who have provided services to the child that she is completely bonded to him and is thriving under his care. The child has been and will continue to be under the care of multiple professionals who will continue to monitor her progress and welfare.

RECOMMENDATIONS

1. That the existing Temporary Guardianship be made permanent.

2. That the recommendation for a psycho-sexual be denied as not being justified as a result of minor's counsel' s assessment.

3. That Petitioner continue to maximize utilization of all resources available to improve the quality of the minor's life and her ability to realize her potential. There has not been a showing that anyone in the child's life is capable of doing more or, for that matter, interested in doing more.

4. That all other existing orders not in conflict with the above remain in full force and effect.

Respectfully submitted,

Alexander C. Verduci, M.S.W., J.D.
LtCol USMC (Ret)
Appointed Minor's Counsel

3

(37)

May 31, 2005

Bonnie Dumanis
San Diego County District Attorney's office
330 W. Broadway
San Diego, CA 92101

Dear Ms. Dumanis:

I am extremely outraged that your office has failed to respond to my letter of May 2, 2005. Attached is a copy for your convenience. It now appears evident that you intend to ignore the actions of Iain R. just as the Deputy District Attorney prosecuting the case against my son Robert Rubino has ignored the admissions of illegal conduct by this witness for over a year.

This child has admitted in great detail his acts of abuse and molestation in this community that are documented back to 1999. He prays on younger children. It is clear from his testimony on March 24, 2005 that he continues to molest younger children.

Not only has he molested other children, it is my understanding that he exposed himself to my great-grandchild, an act that taken alone could be perceived as a childhood prank. However, when you look at his other conduct it cannot be taken lightly. I feel that your office is not taking this matter seriously.

I wrote to you out of concern. I hoped you would take appropriate action. However you have failed to even acknowledge my letter. Based upon the lack of response, I can only assume that nothing will be done in this matter.

I cannot stand by and have the actions of this child covered up because you believe him to be the victim in the case against my son. It appears the District Attorney's office is playing Judge and Jury, making decisions that Iain R.'s victims aren't entitled to the same protections and justice that he is afforded. This is not justice but any means. You have made a conscious choice to do nothing.

I am sure you will try to hide your actions behind statements like you were acting out of the "greater good for the community." But do you think that is how the parents of Iain R.'s future victims will feel? How do you think they will respond when they find out your office could have taken steps to protect their children from this individual and did nothing?

This child needs to be taken off the streets. Someone needs to get him help before he harms someone else. I beg you take appropriate action. If you choose to ignore this letter as you have done the first, I feel that I have no choice but to take this issue to the press. Maybe you will be more responsive to their inquires?

Respectfully submitted,

Lucy Rubino

Lucy Rubino
852 Avenida Ricardo #219
San Marcos, CA 92069
(760) 737-9916

Copies

Carol K. Lackenbach, Esq.
5310 Northwest 1st Avenue
Pompano Beach, Florida 33064

(954) 283-8605

November 25, 2005

Honorable Harry Elias
Judge San Diego Superior Court
Department 25
North Country Division
Vista Regional Center
325 South Melrose
Vista, California 92083

Re: Robert M. Rubino
Hearing Date December 6, 2005

Dear Judge Elias:

I am a New York attorney (presently retired and living in Florida). I have known and represented Robert M. Rubino for approximately twenty years . I know that he has helped many people and that he has been a licensed foster parent and a court appointed guardian for at least thirty years. He has raised approximately thirty-five children. Over the years, I have visited his home in New York, South Carolina, Florida and finally, California. I have met his mother, sister and grandchildren. I have been personally acquainted with many of the children he has helped. These were children whose problems were so severe that no one else would take them in. I am enclosing copies of several letters to Mr. Rubino. These letters were received from courts, schools and probation/parole authorities commending him for his good efforts as reflected in the children's improvement and results. I believe he is a good person who will eventually be found "not guilty" of all charges against him.

I am writing this letter to implore you to reduce his bail to a sum which can be met by Mr. Rubino and his family.

Robert Rubino is sixty-four (64) years old. Because he and his family are unable to post

Page -2-
Honorable Harry Elias

the present bail of Three Million Five Hundred Thousand ($3,500,000.00) Dollars, he has been held in jail, awaiting trial, since October, 2003, more than two years. His health is poor. He has suffered a severe heart attack. He has had angioplasty as well as a triple bi-pass operation. He has had surgery on both knees and he suffers from diabetes and arthritis. I understand that while in jail, he has developed a hernia, possibly because he is unable to climb steps and in order to go upstairs, he has to physically pull himself up the stairs by the handrail. He now needs a wheelchair to get to the courtroom because he can't walk the required distance. To make matters even worse, his mother has advised me that his condition is so deteriorated that with the changing season, he is constantly cold in the jail and that he has to shroud himself with three blankets. She fears his health will further deteriorate and that he will die before his trial can be had..

I most respectfully beg you to reduce the required bail so that he will able to live to be exonerated.

Very truly yours,

Carol K. Lackenbach

CAROL K. LACKENBACH

cc: Richard Layon, Esq.
bcc Larry Rubin

Appendix A: Legal Documents

(Starts on the following page.)

A. On 10/11/22 Judge Brad Weinreb ordered the office of the Public Defender to select a Public Defender Attorney to represent me. As of this date I have had no response or communication nor ever received the name of this attorney who is supposed to represent me. I have not received any legal assistance that I am aware of. In addition this Court denied my request to have Richard Crane C44519 to represent or to communicate directly with me. Therefore I must elect to represent myself, pro se, and proceed legally in spite of my lack of legal knowledge and court procedures. I pray this Court will extend to me some latitude. I am 81 years old, DOB 6/25/41, with numerous serious medical problems. I prefer to attempt my representation before I die unjustly in prison.

B. On or about 2/15/07 Judge Maino unlawfully sentenced me to 225 years in prison for my convictions. This was an unlawful sentence. Approximimately one week later I was recalled to the Court and Maino and prosecutor Clay Biddle both profusely claimed that each was responsible for the unlawful sentence. My conflict attorney, Layon, throughout all these sentencing procedures, said nothing to help me. Next, Maino, in the presence of Biddle and Layon, for a second time unlawfully sentenced me, this time to 73 years plus life in prison. Maino used the new sentencing laws which only a few months earlier in 2006 had become the sentencing laws for crimes which occurred after that 2006 enacted date. All three, Maino, Biddle, and Layon must have known that my alleged 2004 crimes must be sentenced under the sentencing laws in effect in 2003 and that legally I could not be sentenced under the law that went into effect in 2006.

The Appellate Court did state, "If the defendant's attorney had done his job properly, evidence of the defendant's innocence would have been presented to the jury." Layon's silence during these unlawful sentencing procedures is further proof of the blatant refusal to legally protect me even during the obvious willful and malicious unlawful sentencing. To prove to the Court that this second unlawful sentence was a malicious and intentional unlawful sentence I state the following facts.

I filed a 1054.9 petition on 11/4/21 which the Court later granted on 3/22/22, although to date I have never received a copy of that 1054.9 Court order in spite of my several written requests to receive that Court order copy, & again make another such request. The 11/4/21 1054.9 petition was received by Maino who at the time was still my acting Superior Court Judge for my case. In the 1054.9 petition I clearly and fully stated that my sentence imposed by him was unlawful and why it was unlawful. I said that I must be resentenced under the law in effect in 2003 when my alleged crimes were supposed to have occurred and must not be sentenced under the 2006 sentencing laws which did not apply to me and gave me an unlawful life sentence and an excessive prison term. Maino, with full knowledge of the unlawful sentencing of me continued to correct not his unlawful sentence of me with a new correct resentence which applied to me in 2003. By my uncertain estimate of the sentence permitted under 2003 sentencing laws, I estimate that I should have been sentenced to serve about 15 years and no life sentence and with time off for good behavior, etc.

During the 19+ years I have served, I have never been given even one disciplinary 115 violation. I pray that the Court will lawfully resentence me and with consideration for the facts presented in my 1054.9 petition if possible. Also I pray that the Court will order the State to compensate me financially for the actual and punitive damages and suffering I have endured for each and every additional day of incarceration I have served under the malicious and unlawful sentence. I do request the return of all fines, fees and restitution I've paid and with appropriate interest. I do not consider myself a prisoner, I consider myself a hostage of the corrupt judge Maino.

In addition my 1054.9 petition cited numerous serious Brady Violations by Maino. During the months I filed my 1054.9 petition Maino was still my Superior Court acting judge. He had ample opportunity to correct his unlawful sentencing but Maino chose to allow this and other Brady violations to remain in effect in spite of these violations were clearly exposed to him in the 1054.9 petition. Even a second year law school student would recognize that these violations must be corrected and not ignored. I request that this Honorable Court refer these Maino-violations contained within these motions and in the 1054.9 petition for review by the Disciplinary Committee of the Ca. Bar or other appropriate regulatory body.

C. It is my intention in this section C to cite to the Court what I believe constitutes only two of the violations described in the 1054.9 petition which would change my verdict to not guilty in my estimation. Also I request that the Court take judicial notice of all the Brady violations detailed in the 1054.9 petition which the Court granted 3/22/22. Now it is also important to note what is contained in the enclosed

Declaration by Rubino dated 11/4/21 and a part of the 1054.9 petition which the Court granted, tapes 39 and 40 were withheld by the FBI for over 20 years. This concealment of evidence by the FBI constitutes true felony crimes for obstruction of justice for the serious consequences that followed to Rubino's unjust loss of his Foster Care license and more importantly because it was the basis for then FBI Agent Housholder's perjured testimony at Rubino's trial and subsequent false convictions.

The San Diego District Attorney during the past year has confirmed to Rubino that the People recently recovered possession of tapes 39 and 40 from the FBI and the DA will copy these tapes and provide this discovery to Rubino in compliance with the Court's 1054.9 order. Subsequently, as of this date the San Diego District Attorney has now refused to provide the tapes 39 and 40 and all of the 1054.9 discovery order by the Court. At one time they had agreed to provide some of these court order discoveries to Rubino. I request the Court to force the SD-DA to comply and provide all the latest discovery granted by the Court in the 1054.9 petition. As the enclosed Rubino declaration dated 11/4/21 demonstrates, if the defense had these tapes, Rubino would have retained his Foster Care license, would have proved he did not intend to transport for sexual purposes, would have impeded FBI Housholder's fake and perjured testimony at trial and this would have changed the verdicts of Rubino's trial at least in part to not guilty as the 1054.9 cites.

Note Defendant's Motion to Strike People's Amended Response to Defendant's request #15 Pursued to Penal Code Section 1054.9 dated 6/28/22. Also specifically demonstrates that the People have also obstructed justice and, without just cause, have violated this Court's order to produce discovery.

Also note that Defendant's reply to People's Opposition to Defendant's Application pursuant to Penal Code 1054.9 dated July 13, 2022 even with greater specificity proves my above accusation and issues.

These two above Defendant's Motion to Strike and Defendant's Reply to People's Opposition plus the 1054.9 Petition detail that when Judge Elias, for unknown causes, was removed as judge and Maino was secretly selected to replace him, Maino violated the U.S. Supreme Court's order and law which mandate that all discovery favorable to the Defense must be presented to the jury. In violation of the U.S. Supreme Court order, Maino ordered that the jury must not know anything about Iain R's serial sex assaults upon 8 boys ages 3-8 years old plus and Iain R's sodomy of the 6 year old victim's puppy with a stick. Also Iain was not asked if had sex with his pal 9 year old T.J. who is part of the case, because Judge Elias stopped Iain's confession under oath with "How can you bring him (Iain) into my Court?" "The jury will hate him," directed to prosecutor Biddle. Also Maino, a Superior Court judge, does not have the authority to override another Superior Court Judge Elias that these Iain sex crimes must be put in the court record and public knowledge. Even by Maino's own improper jury instruction, by this standard, if the jury knew of Iain R's sex crimes and that Iain was not prosecuted or charged with these crimes in return for his false testimony against Rubino, the concealment of favorable discovery to Rubino would certainly have resulted in a not guilty verdict or verdicts and this constitutes a serious Brady violation. Please also note that in the preliminary court under oath with TJ's mother sitting behind him he stated "It's alright to lie if you have permission." My lawyer Richard Thomas asked him, "What do you mean by that?" and he answered, "If you have to, you can lie to make things go right."

Maino's jury instruction was tailored and stated, "If you believe the victim more than the Defendant, even in the absence of overwhelming evidence, you can find the Defendant guilty." Maino made no mention of the standard instruction that the jury must find the Defendant "guilty beyond a reasonable doubt." Maino's jury instruction violates the Fifth, Sixth and 14th Amendments to the U.S. Constitution. See *In re Winshep* (1970) 397 U.S. 358, 364; *Patterson V. New York* (1977) 432 U.S. 197, 210; *Sandstrom V. Montanna* (1979) 442 U.S. 510, 513; *People V. Flood* (1998) 18C 4th 470, 482; see also *People V. Reyes Martinez,* (1993) 14 CA 4th 1412, 1417.

As in this case Justice delayed has been Justice denied! I make this appeal because in the words of Thomas Jefferson, "Our Cause Is Just."

I, Robert M. Rubino, declare under penalty of perjury that the foregoing is true and correct. Executed 3/22/2023

Robert M. Rubino

Declaration of Robert M. Rubino in support of Post-Conviction Discovery

I, Robert M. Rubino, declare as follows:

1. In 1993 petitioner filed a complaint against FBI agent Robert Householder with the FBI Office of Professional Responsibility alleging Robert Householder was in an illicit homosexual relationship with James Eckenrode a three time convicted child molester, who was also his FBI Confidential Informant. Householder, in retaliation for this complaint petitioner filed, instigated and implemented a malicious and false investigation of the petitioner in revenge for the complaint. Petitioner's complaint resulted in Householder being terminated from the FBI.

2. The results of the complaint and investigation were never produced to the petitioner, and have been suppressed by the FBI. Petitioner repeatedly requested to know the outcome of the investigation, and the facts which were found regarding these allegations. Yet, the results have never been provided, and this evidence would strongly impeach Householder.

3. The FBI told petitioner that, "We are not saying that your accusations are unfounded." "We are continuing to investigate." Without the facts and details about Householder's bad character and abuse of authority, petitioner was denied the right to impeach his testimony.

4. I cared for Walter [redacted] as his foster father and then adopted him, petitioner learned that he had been raped by Eckenrode when he was 7 years old. Petitioner was beyond furious and tried to get proof against Household and Eckenrode. One of Householder's attacks against me forced petitioner to initiate.

at his own expense, a hearing to help keep his foster care license. At an ALJ Hearing, the Judge ruled that petitioner had to be able to prove his innocence, but the Judge ruled that the petitioner was not guilty of any crime. Petitioner was attempting to have two boys to come to California who had been victims of Householder and Eckenrode to testify against them. Yet, these two boys did not exist, but was an undercover Orlando Fla. police officer Rockerfeller.

5. The FBI has two tapes 39 and 40 which contain exculpatory evidence, and proof that the petitioner did not want to engage in any illicit acts as alleged in this case. Further, these two tapes would completely impeach Householder's trial testimony, and prove he testified falsely, in addition to the fact regarding his termination from the FBI which also would impeach him.

6. Householder, FBI agent threatened one of petitioner's (guardian ad litum) children, Russell [redacted] with numerous charges asking him to lie against petitioner, but [redacted] refused to lie; and Judge Johnson threw Householder out of his courtroom and offered to recuse himself due to Householder's improper imfluence.

7. Householder committed a criminal fraud upon the ALJ Court, trial court, and petitioner. With an obsession to prevent the truth about petitioner from being known, he used the power of a federal officer to intimidate, negatively influence, or corrupt facts to falsely and maliciously convict petitioner.

I, Robert M. Rubino, declare under the penalty of perjury that the foregoing is true and correct. Executed Nov., 04, 2021.

Appendix B: Miscellaneous Documents

(Starts on the following page.)

SUMMER STEPHAN
District Attorney
SARA STANINGER, SBN 299560
Deputy District Attorney
330 W. Broadway, Suite 860
San Diego, CA 92101
Tel.: (619) 531-4232
Fax: (619) 515-8632
Email: Sara.Staninger@sdcda.org
Attorneys for the People & Plaintiff

FILED
Clerk of the Superior Court
MAY 26 2022
By: S. Smith

SUPERIOR COURT OF THE STATE OF CALIFORNIA
FOR THE COUNTY OF SAN DIEGO, CENTRAL DIVISION

THE PEOPLE OF THE STATE OF CALIFORNIA, Plaintiff, v. ROBERT RUBINO, Defendant.	Case No.: CN167044 **PEOPLE'S RESPONSE AND OPPOSITION TO DEFENSE MOTION FOR POSTCONVICTION DISCOVERY (PEN. CODE, §1054.9)**

INTRODUCTION

Robert Rubino is an inmate serving a sentence of 73 years to life. In 2006, a jury convicted him of sixteen counts of lewd acts upon a minor, two counts of sending harmful material with intent to seduce a minor. The jury also found true allegations of substantial sexual conduct with a child under fourteen years of age in the commission of the charged offenses, and that the defendant committed the offenses against more than one victim. Petitioner's conviction was affirmed on appeal in 2008. Between 2010 and 2020, Petitioner filed three petitions for writ of habeas corpus in the California Court of Appeal, all of which were denied.

Rubino now seeks postconviction discovery under Penal Code[1] section 1054.9. He requested 25 different categories of discovery.

[1] All further statutory references are to the Penal Code unless otherwise noted.

The People have determined that Rubino is entitled to discovery from eight of the requested categories, and will provide the discovery to Rubino. This discovery consists of FBI Tape Recordings #39 and #40 (Request 10), the Forensic Medical Report (Request 11), Laboratory Service Reports regarding DNA (Request 14), Decision of the Department of Social Services by Administrative Law Judge Lawrence Bolton (Request 15), Partial Transcript of March 19, 1999 Hearing regarding Paul Hamaghi (Request 15), Letters from the Honorable Judge Robert Hammerman (Request 16), Letter from the Honorable Judge Richard Wickersham (Request 17), Letter from Attorney Alexander Verduci (Request 19), and Letters from West Side School of New York City Day Treatment Center (Request 20).

The People request this court deny Rubino's remaining requests for postconviction discovery. The specific objections for each item of discovery are discussed in detail below. In summary, they should be denied for the following reasons:

- Requests 1, 3, 4, 5, 7, 8, 12, 13, 16-22, 24, and 25 should be denied because the requests fail to establish that Rubino would have been entitled to the materials at the time of trial.
- Requests 2, 5, 6, 9, 12, 15, 22, and 23 should be denied because Rubino does not state a reasonable belief that such records exist.
- Requests 6, 7, and 15 should be denied because the prosecution has no duty to create new or duplicate missing or destroyed discovery.
- Requests 12, 15, and 18 should be denied because the request does not identify records with reasonable specificity.
- Request 16-17 and 19-20 should be denied because the requests are overbroad.

RELEVANT PROCEDURAL HISTORY

Following a lengthy jury trial, Rubino was convicted on August 22, 2006, of eighteen counts of lewd acts upon a minor and sending harmful material with intent to seduce a minor in violation of Penal Code sections 288, subdivision (a) and 288.2, subdivision (a); allegations pursuant to Penal Code section 1203.066, subdivision (a)(8) and section 667.62, subdivision

//

//

People v. Flood (1998) 18 C. 4th 470, 482; see also, People v. Reyes Martinez (1993) 14 CA4th 1412, 1417."

Rubino fails to establish that jury instructions are materials he would have been entitled to in discovery at the time of trial; jury instructions are not part of the prosecution's discovery obligations under section 1054.1 or the Constitution. Additionally, the jury instructions provided at trial are likely contained in the Clerk's Transcript, which is in the court's possession, not the possession of the prosecution.

- **Request 9: "All interviews of Ashley [redacted] (brother of Iain [redacted]), conducted by any law enforcement officer regarding the petitioner, including Detective Victoria Redden and a female Sergeant who were conducting all the interviews of the boys in this case. This interview has been concealed from the defense, and when defense counsel Richard Layon asked Julie [redacted] who said she needed permission from prosecutor Clay Biddle. Later, Julie [redacted] said Clay Biddle refused to allow the defense to interview Ashley [redacted] for impeachment evidence against his brother Iain [redacted]. Ashley [redacted] previously told petitioner, that when Iain [redacted] gets into trouble he will lie. See People v. Stewart (2020) 55 Cal.App.5th 755, 769-770.)"**

Rubino fails to establish a reasonable belief that the requested materials exist. Nevertheless, the People reviewed the records for this case and did not locate any interviews of Ashley [redacted].

- **Request 10: "FBI Tape Recordings numbers 39 and 40 which have been, withheld, and proves the petitioner's innocence and impeached FBI Agent Householder's trial testimony. See, U.S. v. Zaragoza-Moreira (9th Cir. 2015) 780 F.3d 971, 980 (bad faith where Homeland Security agent knew the exculpatory value of the video footage and failed to prevent it from being destroyed); U.S. v. Kohring (9th Cir. 2011) 637 F.3d 895, 903-06 (undisclosed police files from investigation into key witness's sexual exploitation of minors material because it show magnitude of witness's incent-ive to cooperate with government and witness's character for truthfulness); Amado v. Gonzalez (9th Cir. 2013) 734 F.3d 936, 942 (citing Brady v. Maryland (1963) 373 US 83."**

The People located Tape Recordings #39 and #40. They are currently being converted to a digital format and a copy will be provided to Rubino.

- **Request 11: "All medical tests and files from examination of the two alleged victims which proved there was no sodomy, and what medical evidence existed to support the charges. See, In re Figueroa (2018) 4 Cal.5th 576, 583."**

IN THE SUPERIOR COURT OF CALIFORNIA

FOR THE COUNTY OF SAN DIEGO

ROBERT M. RUBINO, Petitioner, On Habeas Corpus.	Super. Court Case No. 167044 PETITION FOR WRIT OF HABEAS CORPUS

ROBERT M. RUBINO, No. F-61501
R.J. Donovan Correctional Fac.
480 Alta Road
San Diego, CA 92179
[In pro pria persona]

THE TABLE OF CONTENTS

TABLE OF AUTHORITIES

TABLE OF AUTHORITIES

IN THE SUPERIOR COURT OF CALIFORNIA
FOR THE COUNTY OF SAN DIEGO

ROBERT M. RUBINO, Petitioner, On Habeas Corpus.	Superior Court Case No. 167044 **PETITION FOR WRIT OF HABEAS CORPUS**

TO THE HONORABLE PRESIDING JUDGE OF THE SUPERIOR COURT OF THE COUNTY OF SAN DIEGO, OF THE STATE OF CALIFORNIA:

Petitioner, Robert M. Rubino, hereby petitions for a writ of habeas corpus and by the verified petition states as follows:

I

Petitioner is unlawfully incarcerated and restrained at R.J. Donovan Correctional Facility in San Diego County, California, by Jeff Macomber, Secretary of the California Department of Correction and Rehabilitation, pursuant to a judgment pronounced by the San Diego County Superior Court, in Case No. 167044.

IN THE SUPERIOR COURT OF CALIFORNIA
FOR THE COUNTY OF SAN DIEGO

ROBERT M. RUBINO, Petitioner, On Habeas Corpus.	Superior Court Case No. 167044 **PETITION FOR WRIT OF HABEAS CORPUS**

TO THE HONORABLE PRESIDING JUDGE OF THE SUPERIOR COURT OF THE COUNTY OF SAN DIEGO, OF THE STATE OF CALIFORNIA:

Petitioner, Robert M. Rubino, hereby petitions for a writ of habeas corpus and by the verified petition states as follows:

I

Petitioner is unlawfully incarcerated and restrained at R.J. Donovan Correctional Facility in San Diego County, California, by Jeff Macomber, Secretary of the California Department of Correction and Rehabilitation, pursuant to a judgment pronounced by the San Diego County Superior Court, in Case No. 167044.

II

By information filed in 2006, in the San Diego County Superior Court, petitioner was charged with ten counts of committing lewd acts on Iain [redacted], a child under 14 years of age (Pen.Code, § 288, subd. (a)), and one count of displaying harmful matter to Iain [redacted] with the intent to seduce him (Pen.Code, § 288.2, subd. (a)), six counts of committing lewd acts on Timothy [redacted], a child under 14 years of age (Pen. Code, § 288, subd. (a)), and one count of displaying harmful matter to Timothy [redacted] with intent to seduce him (Pen.Code, § 288.2, subd. (a)).

III

Petitioner was convicted of all counts after a jury trial, and the trial court sentenced petitioner to a total determinate term of 28 years, plus a total consecutive term of 45 years to life, for a aggregate term of 73 years to life.

IV

On July 22, 2008, petitioner's conviction was affirmed on appeal by the Fourth Appellate District, in Case No. D050466.

V

On 11/16/21 petitioner filed a Penal Code section 1054.9, Post-Conviction Discovery Application pursuant to newly amended Penal Code § 1054.9, as was enacted following AB 1987, and made retroactive pursuant to SB 651 (Glazer). Petitioner was seeking post-conviction discovery to prove his innocence to charges, which resulted from false evidence, and suppressed exculpatory Brady material.

VI

On November 16, 2021, petitioner filed Defendant's Post-Conviction Discovery Application Pursuant to Penal Code Section 1054.9. On March 21, 2022, the Court ordered the People to file a Response to petitioner's Pen.Code §1054.9 application. On May 26, 2022, the People's Response and Opposition to Defense Motion for Postconviction Discovery was served on petitioner and filed with the court. On June 15, 2022, People's Amended Response was filed. Petitioner filed "Defendant's Motion to Strike People's Amended Response to Defendant's Request #15 Pursuant to Penal Code section 1054.9. July 19, 2022, Defendant's Reply to People's Opposition to Defendant's Application Pursuant to Penal Code Section 1054.9, was filed.

VII

On October 11, 2022, Honorable Judge Weinreb appointed the Public Defender's Office to assist petitioner with discovery under Pen. Code § 1054.9, following an attempted murder of the petitioner.

VIII

The People eventually provided a March 24, 2005, Reporters Partial Transcript of Oral Proceedings of Testimony of Iain [redacted]'s testimony pursuant to Evidence Code section 402 Hearing, which had been suppressed by the Prosecution. Discovery of July 11, 2000, Partial Transcript of Proceedings; Testimony of Raymond Sims Jr., from Department of Social Services, hearing before Administrative Law Judge, Vallera J. Johnson. September 25, 2000, Proposed Decision, and October 25, 2000, Order adopting the Decision by Lawrence Bolton.

V

Petitioner's imprisonment is unlawful because:

Ground 1:

Petitioner was deprived of his right under the Sixth Amendment to the Constitution of the United States and article I, section 15 of the California Constitution to the effective assistance of counsel before trial, and was thereby prejudiced. Trial counsel was ineffective in that he failed to "properly" object to the removal of Judge Harry Elias immediately after he ruled to admit impeachment testimony of Iain [redacted]. Trial counsel provide ineffective assistance of counsel in not moving to admit the March 24, 2005, in limine testimony of Iain [redacted], for which there was no reasonable basis not to include testimony impeaching Iain [redacted] with numerous sex offenses he committed against children as young a three years old. (Judicial Notice, A.)

Petitioner was deprive of effective assistance of counsel due to counsel's failure to object to prosecutorial misconduct, prosecutor removing Judge Harry Elias immediately after he was ruling to admit very favorable impeachment evidence of Iain [redacted]; which violated the separation of powers doctrine and no competent diligent advocate for the defense would fail to preserve the error for appeal. (Judicial Notice, Exhibit A.)

Petitioner was deprived of effective assistance of counsel, by defense counsel failure to object to admission of Raymond [redacted] (a male prostitute) without moving to impeach him with his prior testimony before Administrative Law Judge, Vallera J. Johnson, finding Raymond [redacted] not credible, as res judicata.

The facts supporting the above ground for relief are as follows:

Petitioner, filed a complaint with the FBI against agent Robert Housholder based on his association with a known pedophile James Echenroad, after petitioner learned that the pedophile Echenroad had committed sodomy of his son Walter [redacted]; and following this complaint Housholder went on a campaign to retaliate against petitioner with a pursuit of false allegations, and influencing young people to lie against the petitioner starting in Florida.

On July 11, 2000, before the Department of Social Services, State of California, a declaration from Robert Housholder was received into evidence at the ALJ Hearing, and contrary to the cover-up orchestrated by Housholder and the prosecution, Robert Housholder and the Prosecutor's Office of San Diego County were acting in privity, which was not established by defense counsel, because he did not properly defend petitioner. See, People v. Rubino, 2008 Cal.App.Unpub.LEXIS 5883 *6: "No Privity." See, Judicially Noticed adjudicative facts, Exhibits B, C, and D.

On March 24, 2005, defense counsel Gerald Blank raised a motion in limine (which petitioner still does not possess), to impeach alleged victim Iain [redacted] with his sex crimes against children, and sodomizing a puppy with a stick (which killed the puppy). Judge Harry Elias stated after the hearing, "How can you bring him into my courtroom, the jury will hate him." This part of the Reporter's Partial Transcript of Oral Proceedings of Testimony of Iain [redacted] still hasn't been provided to petitioner.

Defense counsel did not conduct any investigation, and did not call witnesses, Jason [redacted], Paul [redacted], who testified in petitioner's defense at the ALJ Hearing declaring that the petitioner "did not engage in sexual conduct with one or more minors including but not limited to [redacted] and/or Child #1 ([redacted]), then minors, in 1993." (RJN, Exhibit C, ¶¶ 18-19.

Defense counsel did not investigate or call witnesses who were molested by Iain [redacted] who were named as victims in the March 24, 2005, Evidence Code section 402 hearing of Iain Russell. (RJN, Exhibit A.)

Defense counsel did not call defense witness, Cheyenne [redacted] to prove that Iain [redacted] and Timothy [redacted] downloaded the semi-nude picture of an adult woman using the petitioner's computed, while petitioner was not at home.

October 4, 2021, petitioner wrote defense counsel Richard Layon requesting his client file which included a $100,000, CD-Rom made by prior defense counsel Gerald Blank, and a copy sent to the State Bar was answered on October 28, 2021. Layon never responded to petitioner's request for his client file.

Defense counsel did not move to admit Transcript from the July 11th, 12th, and 13th 2000 hearing by Administrative Law Judge Vallera J. Johnson, and the final order adopting the Findings of petitioner's innocence by Director Lawrence Bolton.

Defense counsel did not object to the prosecutor's closing false argument. (R.T. 2375):

> "This man has molested children for years from the east coast to the west coast. He's been doing it for years. You are being asked to make a decision in this case on two children that he's molested,

> but you heard evidence about many many more children that he's molested."

Defense counsel failed to object to extensive inadmissible, false evidence, based on the witnesses he failed to impeach, or could have had excluded based on double jeopardy or collateral estoppel stemming from the July 11, 12, and 13, 2000, testimony and ruling by the Administrative Law Court.(R.T. 2426):

> "These prior acts, the prior sex acts, the molests of Ray [redacted], Jason [redacted], all we have to do is prove to you by a preponderance of the evidence that those things happened. Then you can use that evidence to convict him of the charges of Iain and T.J. Thats how it works."

During the above argument, defense counsel allowed the prosecution closing argument a preponderance of the evidence standard of guilty, and not the reasonable doubt standard, without objection by defense counsel Richard Layon. (R.T. 2396):

> "Let's talk about the defendant's actions a little bit, why his actions tell you he's guilty. There's the prior molests. The list could go on and on and on. There's Ray [redacted], Jason [redacted]...."

Defense counsel should have interviewed and called Jason [redacted], and/or used his prior testimony from the ALJ Hearing from July 11, 12, 13, 2000.

Defense counsel did not move to admit evidence of Iain [redacted]'s prior sex cimes pursuant to Evidence Code §§ 210, and 351, and did not object the the court's use of Evidence Code § 352, to suppress crucial exculpatory and impeachment evidence.

Defense counsel failed to use Evidence Code § 780 to impeach the credibility of these witness, and abandoned the petitioner's defense.

Ground 2:

Petitioner was denied the right to exculpatory evidence through the police, prosecution, and Federal Bureau of Investigations suppression of evidence of petitioner's innocence to the alleged crimes, and their production of known false evidence.

The facts supporting the above ground for relief are as follows:

Petitioner moved to South Carolina in 1988, purchasing a home formerly owned by the Praise the Lord (PTL), the home in which Jim and Tammy Baker lived. He moved to South Carolina because he had purchased a wholesale pizza business. The house burned to the ground on March 8, 1990. Petitioner had a dispute with State Farm Insurance Company regarding payment of the insurance proceeds for the home. Ultimately, he sued and won a judgment against the insurance company. (RJN, Exhibit C p. 3 ¶7)

FBI Agent Robert L. Housholder conspired with a known child molester, and roommate of Housholder, Jim Echenroad, and Raymond [redacted], an admitted male prostitute to make allegations in this case against him as a result of the civil action against State Farm Ins. Company. In addition, petitioner believed that Echenroad sexually molested [redacted], [redacted], Wally [redacted] and [redacted]. Petitioner's son, and foster care children along with others. (RJN, Exhibit C, pp. 7-8 ¶18.)

On July 11, 12, and 13, 2000, were an administrative hearing before the Administrative Law Judge Vallera J. Johnson, State of California, Office of Administrative Hearings in San Diego, California, where Housholder's declaration was admitted. (RNJ, Exhibit B, page 56 lines 11-14.)

The July 11, 2000, Partial Transcript of Proceedings Testimony of Raymond [redacted], proves that "the FBI," and "a federal law enforcement agency and a local state law enforcement agency in the State of Florida." (RJN, Exhibit B, page 46 ¶2). Were working with the Department of Social Services Legal Division, Alice Jackson-Wright, Senior Staff Attorney, FBI Agent Robert Housholder, and the police in privity with the Department of Social Services. (RJN, Exhibit B, p. 46 ¶2):

> "MS. JACKSON-WRIGHT: Your Honor, several things. I think the foundation has been laid through the witness who has testified that he heard the conversation, is part of the conversation, he made the original tapes, that he made them under the cooperation and direction of both local police agency in Florida and -- a federal law enfocement agency and a local state law enforcement agency in the State of Florida."
>
> "I would additionally indicate -- represent to the Court that California does have a law which is very similar .... California law is Penal Code section 633."

The withheld evidence unequivocally proves that the Department of Social Services were working in privity with police and Federal Bureau of Investigation, through Housholder.

> "MS. JACKSON-WRIGHT: Your Honor, this document -- in this document Agent Housholder does indicate that the tapes that were provided to the Department, the two tapes of the conversation on November 24th, 1997, were provided to the Department -- excuse me -- were originally created as part of an investigation in Jacksonville, Florida, where the originals are kept, and that they were conversations between Ray [redacted] and Robert Rubino." (RJN, Exhibit B, pp. 56-57.)

The Prosecution withheld, and suppressed the involvement of law enforcement with the Department of Social Services to cover-up their involvement and privity between them.

"MS. JACKSON-WRIGHT: Your Honor, I have an item I would like marked which is a declaration of a Special Agent, Federal Bureau of Investigation, Robert L. Housholder." (Exhibit B, p. 56 lines 11-14.)

During the July 2000, hearings before the ALJ Court, "Two of children who have been in his (Petitioner's) care in the past testified in this hearing, [redacted] and [redacted]. [redacted] described respondent (petitioner) as a grandfather figure, while [redacted] considers him like a father. They feel that they can discuss their problems with him openly and honestly, that he will understand and, most significantly, he cares. He has been generous to the boys in many ways and is financially able to do so. Respondent (petition) believes that God has blessed him, and he enjoys helping the children." (RNJ, Exhibit C, p. 11 ¶19.)

The ALJ Judge ruled that, "However, there is uncontested evidence that respondent "(petitioner) has been unable to achieve an erection since 1988. when testifying regarding the facts and circumstances surrounding the misconduct that led to Echenroad's conviction and the investigation thereof, Child #1' demeanor, attitude and testimony changed. He became more defensive and his responses more ambiguous. When he testified regarding the statements to law enforcement officers regarding the sexual incidents with respondent, his testimony was also evasive."

"Considering the factors set forth in the foregoing paragraphs of this Finding 18, among the three witnesses, [redacted] and respondent (petitioner) are more credible that Child #1."

"19. Respondent did not engage in sexual conduct with one or more minors including but not limited to [redacted] and/or

Child #1, then minors, in 1993." (RJN, Exhibit C, ¶¶ 18-19.)

The ALJ Judge made findings on Raymond [redacted] lack of credibility, "Child #1 ([redacted]) testified that he lied when he testified on videotape about the number of times that he had sex with Echenroad while police detectives were present." ¶18.

"Respondent (sic) ([redacted]) made statements on direct-examination that were inconsistent with his testimony on cross-examination regarding the sexual incidents with respondent (Finding 13). Also, his testimony is not only inconsistent with that of [redacted] and respondent on the central issue of whether he had a sexual threesome with [redacted] and respondent but also with [redacted]'s testimony on other matters. Child #1 testified that he hustled with [redacted] on the street, which [redacted] denied this. Child #1 testified that they were good friends until [redacted] moved to California, and [redacted] testified that he did not like Child #1 and stated his reasons therefor (Finding 11)." ¶18.

"Child #1 testified that, during the second and third sexual incidents, i.e., the threesome, respondent achieved an erection and ejaculated. However, there is uncontested evidence that respondent has been unable to achieve an erection since 1988." (RJN, Exhibit C, p. 8, ¶8.)

Futhermore, "There is no evidence that respondent (Rubino) made statements when he testified that are inconsistent with statements that he made on the tape recordings/transcript, i.e., that he made prior inconsistent statements. Therefore, complainant may not attack respondent's credibility." (RJN, p. 9 ¶20, Exhibit C.)

Ground 3:

Petitioner was subjected to Double Jeopardy in violation of the Fifth and Fourteenth Amendments to the United States Constitution and collateral estoppel from the prior trial and judgment before the Administrate Law Court.

The facts supporting the above ground for relief are as follows:

The FBI Agent Robert L. Housholder, was using an informant and roommate Jim Echenroad to arrange for a marijuana buy from Florida to California between Walter [redacted] petitioner's foster son whom he had adopted, and a Russell [redacted] in Florida; and was working with San Diego Police Detective Victoria Reden the California law enforcement. Echenroad and Housholder were in Florida making the taped calls to petitioner's home in San Diego and spoke with petitioner trying to get him involved. Petitioner refused to get involved in any way, and was recorded stating: "I have nothing to do with pot. I hate that shit." These tapes are being withheld from petitioner which prove his innocence of all of these allegations.

In 1999 Walter [redacted] and Russell [redacted] got arrested for the marijuana business, by Victoria Reden and Robert Housholder simultaneously in California and Florida through the San Diego Police and the Federal Bureau of Investigation by Housholder and Detective Reden. Petitioner was never connected to these offenses or charges.

In 1999 (approx.) Petitioner filed a lawsuit against Officer Reden and the San Diego Police Department after they removed two of his children from school and placed in Polinski Center.

The two children brothers Paul and Michael [redacted]. Reden had them crying while trying to force them to lie about petitioner's behavior. Paul called petitioner from Polinski. Petitioner got him attorney Jill Church who filed in family court for Paul, and Judge Bolton emancipated Paul [redacted] at 14 years old.

Detective Reden had the Department of Social Services take petitioner's foster care license; and petitioner filed with the DSS to get his foster care license restored.

Petitioner filed a lawsuit against Detective Reden and the San Diego Police Department in San Diego Superior Court to stop Detective Reden from threatening petitioner son Walter [redacted] and harassment. Petitioner's attorney Richard Thomas got Det. Reden to stop threatening to take Walter [redacted]'s children-settlement of the lawsuit, and petitioner agreed to dismiss the lawsuit.

July 11, 2000, petitioner was in Administrative Law Court before Judge, Vallera J. Johnson, with witnesses Jason [redacted] and Paul [redacted] for his defense; the hearings extended from July 11, 2000, until July 13, 2000, and petitioner was represented by Attorney Richard Thomas.

During the ALJ Hearing, the attorney for DSS brought Raymond [redacted] (roommate of Robert Housholder, and Jim Echenroad) as an alleged victim of sexual misconduct by petitioner, and Raymond [redacted] lied under oath for the purposes of retaliating for both Robert Housholder, and Detective Reden to bring false charges of child molestation against petitioner and send him to prison. The hearings orchestrated by Housholder, Echenroad, and Reden were not successful in bringing the false charges, but out of caution the judge did not restore petitioner's license.

The evidence shows FBI Agent Housholder was acting with the prosecution to frame petitioner; and he attempted to create a charge against petitioner in July 11, 12, and 13, 2000, at the hearing with the Department of Social Services after stalking petitioner from Florida because petitioner had reported him as living with a three time convicted child molester Jim Echenroad. Petitioner's defense counsel Richard Thomas argued in the July 11, 2000, hearing. (Exhibit B, pp. 56-57): "MS. JACKSON-WRIGHT: Your Honor, this document -- in this document Agent Housholder does indicate that the tapes that were provided to the Department, the two tapes of the conversation on November 24th, 1997, were provided to the Department -- excuse me -- were originally created as part of an investigation in Jacksonville, Florida, where the originals are kept, and that they were conversations between Ray [redacted] and Robert Rubino.

And it is a declaration, Your Honor, I would like to submit in support of the admissibility of the tapes. And I do think the statements of Mr. -- I mean the hearsay statements of Mr. [redacted] in this case, I believe, would be sufficient as a foundational matter. THE COURT: Response? MR. THOMAS: Your Honor, this declaration was previously provided; however, there was no notice to this hearing with the ten-day rule that it would be introduced as evidence into this court.

Again, Mr. Housholder, whose name is beginning to come out in this hearing, will become even more of a household word as we progress with the hearing.

This is part of an investigation. If the Court is going to allow these tapes in, then the Respondent should be entitled to the rest of the investigation which was targeted towards Mr. Rubino, because we believe that there is exculpatory evidence in those other tapes." (RJN, Exhibit B, pp. 56-57.)

This withheld evidence shows privity between the prosecution and the Department of Social Services Administrative hearing in which petitioner was exonerated of molestation because the Judge ruled "Respondent (Robert Rubino) did not engage in sexual conduct with one or more minors including and not limited to [redacted] and/or Child #1 (Raymond [redacted]), then minors." (RNJ, Exh. C, p. 8 ¶19, Bates stamped 000205.) This was a conclusive order and judgment by an Administrative Law Judge, and adopted by the Director, Lawrence Bolton, on October 25, 2000. (RJN, Exhibit D.)

The evidence is clear that Agent Housholder attempted to create a charge of child molestation against petitioner at the time of the hearing on July 11, 2000, but the court did not believe the evidence, and ruled for petitioner. (RJN Exh. B-C-D)

The People (Housholder, or Detective Reden) did not file for a writ of mandate or appeal these findings and conclusive orders of Administrative Law Court, and this was withheld exculpatory evidence to frame petitioner on child molestation.

The law required that the People (Government Officials) had to petition to the courts within a statutory time-frame in order for this ruling to not be a permanent judgment; but it was not challenged, and it became res judicata, and a final judgment.

The petitioner was subjected to double jeopardy, and denied exculpatory evidence by the prosecution covering up the evidence and denied effective assistance of counsel in the process.

Ground 4:

Petitioner was denied of his right to Confrontation of the alleged witnesses against him in violation of the Sixth and Fourteenth Amendments to the United States Constitution.

The facts supporting the above ground for relief are as follows:

Petitioner was denied the right to cross-examine Iain [redacted] with the March 24, 2005, record from Judge Harry Elias hearing; and Judge Maino admonished that, "No one shall bring up"the March 24 hearing and Maino cited Evidence Code section 352 many times as his reason. Defense counsel did not object to the suppression of this overwhelming impeachment evidence of the sexual depravity of Iain [redacted]; and being accused of sex crimes against children as young as three years old.

Petitioner was denied the right to show Iain [redacted] was offered immunity from prosecution for these crimes, and he was 15 years old at the time he testified on March 24, 2005, not a child; but a seriously disturbed young man, who even sodomized a puppy with a stick killing the puppy.

Iain [redacted] was accused of sexual crimes against Brook [redacted], petitioner's granddaughter.

Iain [redacted] was accused of sodomy of a three year old child with a stick; and this may have caused a serious injury to the child.

Iain [redacted] stole gameboys and money from petitioner's house, and his apparent sex buddy Timothy [redacted] downloaded semi-nude photographs off the inter-net from petitioner's computer as part of the false charges against petitioner.

In 2003 petitioner was arrested after Detective Reden, and Housholder coerced a young sexual predator Iain [redacted] to make false statements of child molestation against him.

On March 24, 2005, motions in limine pursuant to Evidence Code section 402 where held in Department No. 25, Honorable Harry M. Elias, Judge, was the assigned judge for all purposes; and alleged victim Iain [redacted], testified that he was "15" years old. (Exhibit A, p. 2 line 25) Gerald Blank defense counsel of petitioner's at that time, cross-examined Iain [redacted] based on information that he was accused of molesting numerous younger children, as young as three years old. Id. 52.

During the March 24, 2005, motion under Evidence Code § 402, Judge Harry Elias ruled that he was going to allow impeachment of Iain [redacted] with his prior sex offense against petitioner's granddaughter Brook [redacted] pursuant to Evidence Code section 782; but the prosecution suppressed this order and evidence. (RJN, Exhibit A, pp. 46-47):

> "Q. Was there a time when you exposed your private to Mr. Rubino's granddaughter Brook?"
>
> "MS. RYAN: Objection. Beyond the scope of this hearing and motions yesterday."
>
> "THE COURT: Sustained.
>
> I already indicated that incident would be allowed within the trial itself, so there's no reason to cover it under the 782."
>
> "MR. BLANK: With that, your Honor, I need a break for just a moment."

The prosecution filed a Code of Civil Procedure, section 170.6, and had Judge Harry Elias disqualified to suppress this impeachment evidence against Iain [redacted]'s character.

During the March 24, 2005, hearing pursuant to Evidence Code section 782, Iain [redacted] admitted to molesting a child named David, who was "Like three, four", years younger than he was at the time. (RJN, Exhibit A, pp. 17, 18-28) Including oral copulation, and sodomy. (id. p. 25; 28) Masturbation. (id., pp. 23, 30).

During the March 24, 2005, hearing Iain [redacted] admitted to molesting another child named Garrett. (RJN, Exhibit A, p. 34) Iain [redacted] admitted that Garrett "tried to resist" him, and he "Just convinced him." (Exhibit A, p. 36.) Iain [redacted] said: "No. He touched my -- butt and stuff. That's what we did." (Exhibit A, p. 37)

During the March 24, 2005, hearing Iain [redacted] admitted he shot "Garrett with a BB gun", "In the butt." (Exh. A, p. 47) Iain [redacted] testified that Garrett "was three years old." (Exh. A, p. 52, line 23.)

March 24, 2005, Iain [redacted] was cross-examined regarding a report that read, "that Garrett says you put a stick in his poe poe (phonetic?" And, Iain [redacted] did not deny he had done this, but responded "I just don't remember." Not that it did't happen. "A. Yes." (Exhibit A, p. 55)

All of these sexual offenses committed by Iain [redacted] were suppressed by the prosecution; and petitioner was denied the right to impeach his character with these actions.

This deprived petitioner of cross-examination on Iain [redacted]'s character for truthfulness, and bad character, and deprived petitioner of a fair trial.

GROUND 5:

Petitioner was sentenced to life in prison in violation of Ex Post Facto Clause of the United States Constitution based on Penal Code statutes which were no in effect at the time the alleged crimes occurred.

The facts supporting the above ground for relief are as follows:

Petitioner filed a petition for writ of habeas corpus with this Honorable Court on this issue, and without adequate knowledge of the law; but under great emotional distress as an 81 year old man being victimized by young prisoners, and after having suffered an attempted murder by similar violent prisoners and filed an inadequate petition for writ of habeas corpus in desperation to obtain freedom from the false imprisonment he is suffering.

January 10, 2024, the court denied the petition for writ of habeas corpus; and petitioner prays that the court shall reconsider this ruling.

VI .

Petitioner hereby incorporates by reference the accompanying Motion for Judicial Notice pursuant to Evidence Code, section 451, et seq., the accompanying memorandum and declaration(s) contained in the appendices attached hereto. Petitioner's claims in this petition will be based on the petition, the accompanying Motion for Judicial Notice, the accompanying memorandum, the attached declaration(s), and all records, documents produced or requested during Petitioner's Post-Conviction Discovery Application; plus, all records, documents, pleadings on file with this Court and the petitioner's direct appeal and any further material to be developed at any future hearing that may be ordered.

VII

Petitioner hereby requests that this Court take judicial notice of the record in petitioner's prior direct appeal and the briefs filed and lodged with the Court of Appeal in Case No. D050466, decided on July 22, 2008, by the Court of Appeal (Evidence Code, §§ 451, 452, 459, et seq.). Reproducing the record for use in connection with this petition would entail unnecessary expense since the Court and Respondent already have a copy of the record and all pleadings in archives.

Petitioner further requests the Court take judicial notice of the fact that petitioner is the Godfather of Christopher Wray, Director of the FBI, and brothers Michael Wray, Sean Wray, sister Rosie Wray, children of father Vernon Wray and mother Anna Wray, pursuant to Evid. Code §452(c), public record of baptism in support of petitioner's good character.

VIII

Petitioner hereby requests that this Court take judicial notice of the records filed and lodged with this court on this Case No. SCN167044, Reporter's Partial Transcript of Oral Proceedings, of Testimony of Iain [redacted], March 24, 2005, before Honorable, Harry M. Elias, Judge; the Partial Transcript of Proceedings Testimony of Raymond [redacted], July 11, 2000, from San Diego, California, Department of Social Services State of California, the Honorable, Vallera J. Johnson, Administrative Law Judge, In the Matter of Robert Rubino, No. 379905301; L-2000050158, consisting of 3 cover pages, and pages 41 through 75; and the Proposed Decision, of Vallera J. Johnson, Administrative Law Judge, dated September 25, 2000, and the Decision, by Lawrence Bolton, Deputy Director, Legal Division, dated October 25, 2000, attached, adopting the decision of Vallera J. Johnson. Concurrently filed with this Petition for Writ of Habeas Corpus by Motion for Judicial Notice pursuant to Evidence Code, section 451, et seq., Exhibits A, B, C, and D.

WHEREFORE, petitioner respectfully requests that this Court:

1. Take judicial notice of the records in the above and incorporated Motion for Judicial Notice consolidated for purpose of Petition for Writ of Habeas Corpus;

2. Order respondent to show cause why petitioner is not entitled to the relief sought;

3. Conduct an evidentiary hearing to answer the factual questions necessary to determine the merits of petitioner's claims;

4. Appoint counsel to assist the petitioner in the further presentation of his claims for relief;

5. After full consideration of the issues raised by this petition, grant the petition, vacate the February 22, 2007, sentence and judgment of conviction of the San Diego County Superior Court in Case No. 167044; and

6. Grant such other and further relief as may seem just under the circumstances.

Date: April _7_, 2004.

Respectfully submitted,

Robert M. Rubino

Robert M. Rubino

Verification

I, Robert M. Rubino, declare under the penalty of perjury that the foregoing is true and correct.

Dated: April _7_, 2024.

Robert M. Rubino

Robert M. Rubino

MEMORANDUM

I

PETITIONER WAS DEPRIVED OF EFFECTIVE ASSISTANCE OF BOTH TRIAL COUNSEL, AND APPELLATE COUNSEL DUE TO THE PROSECUTION'S SUPPRESSION OF EXCULPATORY EVIDENCE IN VIOLATION OF THE 6TH AND 14TH AMENDMENTS TO THE U.S. CONSTITUTION

The prosecution suppressed Brady material, and these actions deprived petitioner of both effective assistance at trial; and effective assistance of appellate counsel. See, In re Hampton (3rd Dist. 2020) 48 Cal.App.5th 463, 474:

> "The same cannot be said of his IAAC claim. For obvious reasons, such a claim could not have been raised on appeal. As our Supreme Court has observed, where a claim was available on direct appeal, but not raised due to ineffective assistance of appellate counsel, such a claim is "cognizable in a postappeal habeas corpus petition under the ineffective counsel rubic." (In re Harris (1993) 5 Cal.4th 813, 834 ... see also, In re Banks (1971) 4 Cal.3d 337, 343 ... In re Spears (1984) 157 Cal.App.3d 1203, 1208 ... ["habeas corpus is the appropriate means to remedy deprivation of the effective assistance of appellate counsel"].)."

Petitioner's habeas claims raised herein did not become cognizable until the prosecution produce some of the suppressed Brady material in response to petitioner's Penal Code §1054.9 application; and, the government has still failed to produce an abundance of other Brady material. Brady v. Maryland (1963) 373 U.S. 83; Napue v. Illinois (1956) 360 U.S. 264, 269.

The petitioner's original appellate counsel was rendered ineffective by the governments withholding substantial favorable evidence at trial; and counsel provided ineffective assistance by not objecting to the withholding of evidence. See, People v. Rubino, 2008 Cal.App.Unpub. LEXIS 5883, page 36:

> "Although Mullens involved a jury verdict acquitting the defendant of a charge involving propensity evidence and this case involves an administrative finding by the ALJ that Rubino did not engage in sexual conduct with Raymond S. and Jason B., that factual difference is not conclusive and would have caused the trial court in this case to conclude our holding in Mullens was inapplicable. Rather, on reading our reasoning in Mullens, the trial court would likely have concluded Mullens applied to permit admission of evidence of the ALJ's finding to rebut the prosecutor's propensity evidence involving the same minors."

The appellate court in petitioner's original direct appeal, was without all of the evidence; and, trial counsel's totally incompetent failure to consult with petitioner, or object to the suppression of the ALJ's favorable ruling, and prosectorial misconduct in removing Judge Harry Elias in order to suppress the March 24, 2005, testimony of Iain [redacted], which was raised by competent advocacy of attorney Gerald Blank, petitioner's counsel at the time in a 402 hearing. See, Delgado v. Lewis (9th Cir. 2000) 223 F.3d 976, 982 ("In Delgado I we concluded that "absent a reasoned explanation, federal courts are left simply to speculate about what 'clearly established law' the state court might have applied." Delgado I, 168 F.3d at 1152. Thus, we accordingly concluded that, in such circumstances, the state court decisions do "not warrant the deference we might usually apply" and that "the district court properly deduced that it was left with no alternative but to review independently the claims of the petition." Id. at 1152-53." "... The record before us, the same record before the California Court of Appeal and Supreme Court reveals a total failure of the legal system to provide even a modicum of acceptable representation to Delgado.").

The Sixth Amendment guarantees the right to effective assistance of counsel in criminal prosecutions. See, Yarborough v. Gentry (2003) 540 U.S. 1, 5 (per curiam); similar case People v. Zaheer (4th Dist.2020) 54 Cal.App.5th 326, 339 ("It is, rather the combined effect of defense counsel's failure to establish a critical predicate fact and the prosecutor's decision to take advantage of omission that we consider. Evaluating these issues together, it is clear that the prosecutor's argument, whether erroneous or not, was made possible by and flows directly from defense counsel's earlier mistake. But for that oversight, the prosecutor would have been unable to advance her misleading suggestion. Against that backdrop, we proceed to evaluate the full consequences of defense counsel's omission.").

The court in Zaheer makes an appropriate argument, "Here, however, the combined effect of defense counsel's failure to establish a necessary predicate fact and the prosecutor's exploitation of that omission collectively deflected a substantial reason to doubt Martha's story. We consider this chain of events because prejudice is a contextual inquiry that examines the actual effect of defense attorney's error on the trial outcome. (See, e.g., In re Jones (1996) 13 Cal.4th 552, 586 [54 Cal.Rptr. 2d 52, 917 P.2d 1175] [prosecutor's exploitation in closing argument of an evidentiary gap left by defense counsel demonstrated why "defense counsel's deficient performance as to this issue clearly was significant"]; see also Strickland, supra, 466 U.S. at p. 691 [the focus of the prejudice analysis is whether the error affected the judgment].)." People v. Zaheer, 54 Cal. App.5th 326, 339.

Trial counsel was ineffective in failing to move to admit the ALJ's factual findings, and proposed decision and final decision, which held that, "Considering the factors set forth in the foregoing paragraphs of this Finding 18, among the three witnesses, [redacted] and respondent (Robert Rubino) are more credible that Child #1 (Raymond [redacted]). 19. Respondent (Robert Rubino) did not engage in sexual conduct with one or more minors including but not limited to [redacted] and/or Child #1 (Raymond [redacted]), then minors, in 1993." (Exhibit B, pg. 8 ¶¶18-19.) See, People v. Rubino, 2008 Cal.App.Unpub.LEXIS 5883 *22:

> "Rubino contends the trial court erred by excluding evidence on the ALJ's finding at the prior DSS administrative hearing that he did not engage in sexual conduct with Raymond S. and Jason B. in 1993. However, Rubino concedes his trial counsel did not expressly request that the ALJ's finding be admitted in evidence."

The appellate court ruled that, "a reviewing court will not consider an appellate contention ... where an objection could have been, but was not, made in the trial court," citing People v. Saunders (1993) 5 Cal.4th 580, 589-590, and other authority. People v. Rubino, supra, *24. Further, the appellate court ruled "Rather, we conclude that had Rubino offered evidence of the ALJ's finding and adequately argued in favor of its admissility, the trial court would likely have admitted that evidence despite any initial section 352 concerns. At the time of Rubino's trial, there was case law that would have influenced the trial court to admit evidence of the ALJ's finding had Rubino offered it. In People v. Mullens (2004) 119 Cal.App.4th 648 (Mullens), we summarized the "Griffin rule:" "In sum,

[People v. Griffin (1967) 66 Cal.2d 459], and its progeny, ... the trial court must also allow the defense to present evidence of the defendant's acquittal, if any, of such crimes, and failure to allow such acquittal evidence constitutes error. [Citations.]" (Mullens, supra, 119 Cal.App.4th at pp. 664-665.) In Mullens, we concluded the Griffin rule applied in a sex offense case in which the trial court admitted section 1108 propensity evidence offered by the prosecutor showing the defendant had committed an uncharged sex offense. (Mullens, supra, 119 Cal.App.4th at pp. 665-669.) .... defendant was acquitted of that offense." Mullens, supra, 119 Cal.App.4th at p. 665.)." Petitioner's defense counsel discussed the Mullens case after, "The trial court then asked Rubino's counsel: "What about the Mullens[] case?" People v. Rubino, p. *35.

Wherefore, the appellate court ruled, "Based on the record in this case, because Rubino (counsel) did not offer in evidence the ALJ's finding and such an offer would have been futile, we conclude Rubino waived or forfeited his contention on appeal that the trial court erred by excluding that evidence." id. *37.

A. Request for Judicial Notice

Petitioner's is requesting judicial notice of the prior appeal in People v. Rubino, 2008 Cal.App.Unpub.LEXIS 5883, as a part of the record in this case, and in support of ineffective assistance of counsel. See, Deschene v. Pinole Point Steel Co. (1999) 76 Cal.App.4th 33, 37 [count on its own motion took judicial notice of prior opinion]); also, Dwan v. Dixon (1963) 216 Cal.App.2d 260, 265 [Judicial notice of contents of record]

II

PETITIONER WAS DENIED EXCULPATORY EVIDENCE BY BY PROSECUTOR'S SUPPRESSION OF IMPEACHMENT EVIDENCE IN VIOLATION OF DUE PROCESS AND BRADY V. MARYLAND (1963) 373 U.S. 83

On March 24, 2005, petitioner's counsel (Gerald Blank) had an Evidence Code §402 motion brought to impeach Iain [redacted], an alleged victim, to show he was incredible and unbelievable. (RJN, Exhibit A, March 24, 2005, Testimony of Iain [redacted]).

The March 24, 2005, testimony of Iain [redacted] proved that he was an admitted sexual predator of young children, and that he had committed numerous sex offenses against children, and committed oral copulation, and sodomy of the children. (RJN, Exhibit A pg. 52: "Yeah. He was 3 years old.")

Following the testimony of Iain [redacted], presiding judge, Harry Elias stated: "How can you bring him into my courtroom! The jury will hate him." This was impeachment evidence, which could possibly have allowed for a defense motion to strike or exclude his testimony against petitioner, or dismiss the charges against petitioner. See, Evid.Code, §402(c); also see, In re Pratt (2nd Dist.1999) 69 Cal.App.4th 1294, 1299 ("The basis for the ruling was that, under Brady v. Maryland (1963) 373 U.S. 83 [83 S.Ct. 1194, 10 L.Ed.2d 215], Pratt had been deprived of evidence at his 1972 murder trial that would have "permitted potentially devastating cross-examination or other impeachment evidence" regarding prosecution witness Julius Butler, and that this deprivation undermined confidence in the verdict."); and In re Miranda (2008) 43 Cal.4th 541, 546 ("... had used these undisclosed facts to pressure ... into testifying against....").

A. **Prosecutorial Misconduct to Remove Judge Elias**

The prosecution apparently filed a peremptory challenge to remove Judge Harry Elias, pursuant to Code of Civil Procedure, 170.6, following the March 24, 2005, testimony of Iain [redacted], which amounts to a separation of powers violation, and was used to suppress the Brady evidence petitioner had the right to. See People v. Superior Court (Tejeda) (4th Dist.2016) 1 Cal.App.5th 892, 923 ("The California Constitution is 'the supreme law of our state' [citation], subject only to the supremacy of the United States Constitution. (Cal.Const., art. III, § 1.)" (California Logistics, Inc. v. State of California (2008) 161 Cal.App.4th 242, 250 ... It is axiomatic that all statutes, including section 170.6, must be applied in a manner which is consistent with the California and United States Constitutions. The separation of powers clause of the California Constitution divides the powers of the state government into three branches, and dictates that "[p]ersons charged with the exercise of one power may not exercise either of the others except as permitted by this Constitution." (Cal.Const., art. III, §3.).")

B. **Judge Maino acted as an Appellate Court**

The prosecutor had petitioner's case reassigned to Judge Maino, and the judge immediately overruled Judge Elias ruling, and ordered defense counsel not to raise the prior testimony of Iain [redacted], in violation of Supreme Court precedent in Davis v. Alaska (1974) 415 U.S. 308, 316 ("Cross-examination is the principle means by which the believability of a witness and the truth of his testimony are tested.")

The actions of the prosecutor, and Judge Maino endorsing the "Judge shopping" following the March 24, 2005, Evidence Code § 402 hearing to impeachment Iain [redacted], or allow the defense to move for a dismissal based on Iain [redacted]'s admission to numerous sex crimes against children, violated the Petitioner's rights to due process. See, Paul Blanco's Good Car Co. Auto Group v. Superior Court (1st Dist.2020) 56 Cal.App.5th 86, 99:

> "As a general rule, a trial judge cannot over turn the order of another trial judge. (E.g., In re Marriage of Oliverez (2015) 238 Cal.App.4th 1242 1248 .... Ziller Electronics Lab GmbH v. Superior Court (1988) 206 Cal.App.3d 1222, 1232 ......
> Weighty concerns compel the long standing principle. (In re Alberto (2002) 102 Cal.App.4th 421, 426-431 .... Fundamentally, it "is founded on the inherent difference between a judge and a court and is designed to ensure the orderly administration of justice." (Id. at p. 427.) Because the superior court is a single entity comprised of member judges, "'one member of that court cannot sit in review on the actions of another member of that same court.'" (Id. at pp. 427-428.) "For one superior court judge, no matter how well intended, even if correct as a matter of law, to nullify a duly made, erroneous ruling of another superior court judge places the second judge in the role of a one-judge appellate court," and "it would be only a matter of days until we would have a rule of man rather than a rule of law.'" (Id. at p. 427.) Furthermore, to countenance such a practice would lead to judge-shopping-venturing from judge to judge until a favorable ruling is obtained-which "'would instantly breed lack of confidence in the integrity of the courts.'" (Ibid.)."

The Court of Appeal Paul Blanco's Good Car, ruled that, "Accordingly, based on the record, Judge Reilly (Maino) exceeded his authority...." (ibid. p. 102) and vacated the order as being "invalid." (Ibid.) See also, Lees v. Russell (9th Cir. 2023) 75 F.4th 1009, 1012; Martinez v Ryan (2012) 566 U.S. 1.

III

PETITIONER'S RIGHT NOT TO BE SUBJECTED TO DOUBLE JEOPARDY IN VIOLATION OF THE FIFTH AMENDMENT WAS DENIED IN VIOLATION OF ASHE V. SWENSON (1970) 397 U.S. 436

The prosecution's use of testimony from Raymond [redacted], Jason [redacted], and Robert Housholder violated collateral estoppel law, and the testimony subjected petitioner to double jeopardy. See, Stringfield v. Superior Court (S.D.Cal.2016) 166 F.Supp.1144

A. Collateral Estoppel

> "The doctrine of collateral estoppel applies to criminal cases through the Fifth Amendment protection against double jeopardy. Ashe v. Swenson, 397 U.S. 436, 443-46,90 S.Ct. 1189, 25 L.Ed.2d 469 (1970). The Supreme Court in Ashe held that "[w]here a previous judgment of acquittal was based upon a general verdict," and where a defendant seeks to invoke the collateral estoppel doctrine to bar a subsequent prosecution regarding a particular issue, a court is required "to 'examine the record of a prior proceeding, taking into account the pleadings, evidence, charge, and other relevant matter, and conclude whether a rational jury could have grounded its verdict upon an issue other than that which the defendant seeks to foreclose from consideration.'" Id. at 444 (citation omitted)."

On July 11, 2000, Administrative Law Judge, Vallera J. Johnson, conducted a hearing wherein Raymond [redacted] testified, and a Declaration of Robert Housholder, was admitted as Exhibit 74. (RJN, Exhibit B, p. 2.) The hearing was held on July, 11, 12, and 13. On September 25, 2000, Judge Johnson ruled in relevant part, paragraph: "19. Respondent (Robert Rubino) did not engage in sexual conduct with one or more minors including but not limited to [redacted] and/or Child#1 (Raymond [redacted]), then minors, in 1993." (RJN, Exhibit C, pg. 8, ¶19.) On October 25, 2000, Lawrence Bolton, Deputy Director, adopted the decision. (Exh. D)

This was a final judgment, which must be given res judicata effect, because it was not challenged by review, or overturned. See, Balasubramaniam v. Los Angeles County (2d Dist.2000) 78 Cal. App.4th 286, 301 ("A state court may give preclusive effect to an unreview administrative determination.") The aggrieved party, needed to file for review to challenge the final judgment. Cal. Code Civil Proced., § 1094.5. See also, Murray v. Alaska Airlines Inc. (2010) 50 Cal.4th 860, 864 ("The doctrine of collateral estoppel, or issue preclusion, is firmly embedded in both federal and California common law. It is grounded on the premise that "once an issue has been resolved in a prior proceeding, there is no further factfinding function to be performed." (Parkland Hosiery Co. v. Shore (1979) 439 U.S. 322, 336, fn. 23....").

B. Privity Existed in this Case

The withheld evidence and privity between Housholder, [redacted], and San Diego Detective Victoria Reden for years, was concealed by the prosecution to support admission of testimony of Raymond [redacted], Jason [redacted] (notwithstanding suppression of March 24, 2005, testimony of Iain [redacted]). See, Balasubramaniam, supra, at p. 303 ("Privity exist where the person involved is "' ... so identified in interest with another that he represents the same legal right.'" [Citation.] (Armstrong v. Armstrong (1976) 15 Cal. 3d 942, 951, 126 Cal.Rptr. 805, 544 P.2d 941.) Persons in privity with parties subject to a judgment are bound by the same ruling. (ibid.)." "Having concluded that the trial court erred in failing to apply res judicata to preclude relitigation of issues ...." Id. p. 305.

C. Suppressed Evidence would prove Prosecutor Acted In Privity and was Collaterally Estopped from using Raymond [redacted] and Jason [redacted] as prior crime

The trial court erred in admitting testimony from both Raymond [redacted] and, Housholder, to allege petitioner committed prior uncharged sex offense; because these matters were resolved in the Petitioner's favor in July 11, 2000, administrative proceeding before Administrative Law Judge, Vallera J. Johnson, decided in Petitioner's favor on September 25, 2000, and adopted by October 25, 2000, decision of Lawrence Bolton, Deputy Director, Legal Division of the Department of Social Services. See, Exhibits B, C, D. See, People v. Curiel (2023) 15 Cal.5th 433, 451:

> "In general, whether a prior finding will be given conclusive effect in a later proceeding is governed by the doctrine of issue preclusion, also known as collateral estoppel." (Strong, supra, 13 Cal.5th at p. 715.)."

The prosecution's use of testimony from Raymond [redacted] and Housholder , to establish a contrary ruling from the previous ruling in Petitioner's favor by the ALJ court, violated the Petitioner's right to be free from double jeopardy. See, Ashe v. Swenson (1970) 397 U.S. 436, 443:

> "Collateral estoppel" is an awkward phrase, but it stands for an extremely important principle in our adversary system of justice."

The U.S. Supreme Court in Ashe v. Swenson, 397 U.S. 436, 445 stated further, "The ultimate question to be determined, then, in the light of Benton v. Maryland, supra, is whether this established rule of federal law is embodied in the Fifth Amendment guarantee against double jeopardy. We do not hesitate to hold that it is."

The prosecutor with the approval of the trial court argued a lesser standard of guilt, preponderance of the evidence standard, and used knowing false testimony of all of the alleged victims. See, People v. Cowan (2nd Dist.2017) 8 Cal.App 5th 1152, 1159: ("It is improper for the prosecutor to misstate the law, and in particular to attempt to reduce the People's burden of proof beyond a reasonable doubt. (People v. Marshall (1996) 13 Cal.4th 799, 831 [55 Cal.Rptr.2d 347, 919 P.2d 1280]) Improper comments violate the federal Constitution when they constitute a pattern of conduct so egregious that it infects the trial with such unfairness that it denies the defendant due process. (People v. Hill (1998) 17 Cal.4th 800, 819 [72 Cal. Rptr.2d 656, 952 P.2d 673].) Even where improper comments fall short of the test, they may constitute misconduct under state law if they involve the use of deceptive or reprehensible methods in an attempt to persuade the court or jury. (ibid.).") See also, People v. Azcona (6th Dist.2020) 58 Cal.App.5th 504; People v. Collins (5th Dist.2021) 60 Cal.App.5th 540; People v. Medellin (5th Dist.2020) 45 Cal.App.5th 519.

Furthermore, in petitioner's case the court instructed the jury on a lesser standard of guilt, and both the prosecutor and court allowed exculpatory evidence to be suppressed. (Exh. A, pp. 46-47): "THE COURT: Sustained. I already indicated that incident would be allowed within the trial itself, so there's no reason to cover it under the 783." Prosecutor and court suppressed this and the evidence from the entire March 24, 2005 hearing; and the Administrative Law Trial.

On April 10, 2008, the Ninth Circuit issued a published opinion requesting that the Supreme Court of California decide a question of California law. Murray v. Alaska Airlines, Inc., 522 F.3d 920, 923:

> "Under California law, even when the "traditional" threshold requirements of collateral estoppel are met, preclusive effect will not be given to a previously litigated issue unless the public policy underlying the collateral estoppel doctrine would be furthered by doing so."

The California Supreme Court answered the Ninth Circuit's certified question, "The doctrine of collateral estoppel, or issue preclusion, is firmly embedded in both federal and California common law. It is grounded on the premise that "once an issue has been resolved in a prior proceeding, there is no further factfinding function to be performed." (Parkland Hosiery Co. v. Shore (1979) 439 U.S. 322, 336, fn. 23 [58 L.Ed.2d 552, 99 S.Ct. 645].) "Collateral estoppel ... has the dual purpose of protecting litigants from the burden of relitigating an identical issue with the same party or his privy and of promoting judicial economy by preventing needless litigation." (id. at p. 326, fn. omitted.)." Murray v. Alaska Airlines, (2010) 50 Cal.4th 860, 864.

The Supreme Court affirmed the issue petitioner asserts, that "It is settled that the doctrine of collateral estoppel or issue preclusion is applicable to final decisions of administrative agencies acting in a judicial or quasi-judicial capacity." (See Astoria Federal S. & L.Assn. v. Solimino (1991) 501 U.S. 104, 107 [115 L.Ed.2d 96, 111 S.Ct. 2166] [extending the doctrine to the final adjudications of both state and federal agencies]; United States v. Utah Constr.Co. (1966) 384 U.S. 394, 421-422 [16 L.Ed.2d 642, 86 S.Ct. 1545 (Utah Constr.Co.); People v. Sims (1982) 32 Cal.3d 468, 479 [186 Cal.Rptr. 77, 651 P.2d 321] (Sims)...." Similarly to petitioner's case, Sims involved, having been exonerated of a criminal offense by the Department, "who has been exonerated of fraud charges in an administrative hearing conducted by the Department of Social Services is subsequently prosecuted in a criminal proceeding for the same alleged misconduct. The most significant issue is whether the doctrine of collateral estoppel bars the prosecution from re-litigating in the criminal proceeding issues that were previously resolved in the administrative hearing." People v. Sims 32 Cal.3d 468, 472-473.

In Sims, the "hearing officer concluded that DSS did have jurisdiction ... and that the County failed to meet its burden," ... The director of the DSS adopted the fair hearing ... The County did not file with the director a request for a rehearing, nor did it seek judicial review of the decision." ibid. 474.

The court in Sims, affirmed the trial court's dismissal of the criminal case stating, "... collateral estoppel bars the state from prosecuting respondent for welfare fraud since she was exonerated in a DSS hearing of that charge. The DSS was "acting in a judicial capacity and [resolving] disputed issues of fact properly before it which the parties ... had an adequate opportunity to litigate." United States v. Utah Constr. Co., supra, 384 U.S. at p. 422 [16 L.Ed.2d at p. 661].)." People v. Sims, supra, pp. 489-490. Furthermore, "the district attorney's" and the "County" "same government are in privity...." id. 487.

In 2001, following the ALJ Hearing, petitioner was in the San Diego juvenile court with attorney Jill Church, emancipating Paul [redacted], and Judge Bolton granted his emancipation, and he referred to the prior ALJ hearing from 2000, and Judge Bolton said: "I reviewed the ALJ transcripts finding you innocent Mr. Rubino. I am sorry for what you went through." Yet, the evidence was not admitted at trial, but Housholder and [redacted] perjury was. See, In re Benavides (2018) 4 Cal.5th 576, 588 ("A writ of habeas corpus may be prosecuted" where "[f]alse evidence that is substantially material or probative on the issue of guilt or punishment was introduced against a person at a hearing or trial relating to his or her incarceration." (§ 1473, subd. (b)(1).)."

Both Raymond [redacted] and Robert Housholder testified in the petitioner's criminal trial; and false Evidence Code § 1108 was used from the ALJ Hearing; while [redacted] and Housholder could not be impeached by petitioner, and committed perjury, in violation of Brady v. Maryland. See, People v. Stewart, 55 Cal.App.5th 755, 784-785:

> "In our view, the suppression of that evidence compromises the fairness of defendant's trial to a degree that undermines confidence in the result."

The trial court clearly violated petitioner's right to a fair trial, "Because the exclusion of this evidence violated (Petitioner's) right to confront a witness against him under the federal and state constitutions. (U.S.Const., 6th amend.; Cal.Const., art. I, § 15; see Delaware v. Van Arsdall (1986) 475 U.S. 673 .... and on this record cannot be considered harmless beyond a reasonable doubt (Chapman v. California (1967)

386 U.S. 18 .... we will reverse the convictions and sentences, and remand for a new trial." People v. Castaneda-Prado (1st Dist. 2023) 94 Cal.App.5th 1260, 1267.

Similarly to petitioner's case, Castaneda-Prado, was denied the right to cross-examine a child concerning impeachment type motive to falsely accuse the defendant. Castaneda-Prado, supra, 1278-1279.

IV

PETITIONER WAS DEPRIVED OF HIS SIXTH AMENDMENT RIGHT TO CONFRONTATION IN VIOLATION OF THE SIXTH AND FOURTEENTH AMENDMENTS

The petitioner was denied his Sixth and Fourteenth Amendment right to cross-examine prosecution witnesses with their prior testimony, in order to prove Iain [redacted] was an admitted child molester, who with [redacted] downloaded simi-nude photo(s) off of petitioner's computer with Iain [redacted]. Raymond [redacted] was a male prostitute, and Jason [redacted] had committed male prostitution after being enlisted by Raymond [redacted]. (RJN, Exhibit C, p. 4 ¶1)

> "Sixth Amendment Protection of Cross-Examination
>
> (1) Cross-examination is known as "'the greatest legal engine ever invented for the discovery of truth.'" (White v. Illinois (1992) 502 U.S. 346, 356 [116 L.Ed.2d 848, 112 S.Ct. 736].) "Subject always to broad discretion of a trial judge to preclude repetitive and unduly harassing interrogation," the United State Supreme Court has said, "[c]ross-examination is the principal means by which the believability of a witness and the truth of his testimony are tested." (Davis v. Alaska (1974) 415 U.S. 308, 316 [39 L.Ed.2d 347, 94 S.Ct. 1105] (Davis)." Castaneda-Prado, supra, 1278-1279.

Further, what type of immunity was granted to these alleged witnesses, or payment. In re Pratt, 69 Cal.App.4th 1294, 1307-08.

The fact that FBI Agent Housholder was living with Raymond [redacted], and Jim Echenroad in Florida proves a connection in the false prosecution of petitioner even before California; and Housholder's personnel file is essential to prove petitioner's complaint, and Housholder's record of misconduct for impeachment purposes. See, People v. Sons (2nd Dist. 2008) 164 Cal.App.4th 90, 92 ("By stipulation, this conviction was vacated in the United States District Court because former prosecutor intentionally withheld discovery concerning Officer Maxwell's previous disciplinary record. (See Brady v. Maryland (1963) 373 U.S. 83, 86 .... (originally sentenced to) "life without the possibility of parole. ... having killed California Highway Patrolman Richard Maxwell." ibid. "The prosecutor's conduct concerning the officer's disciplinary record was deplorable and condemned by the previous Court of Appeals. (Sons v. Superior Court, supra, 125 Cal.App.4th at p. 119.)." id. 99, fn. 6.

After obtaining Officer Maxwell's personnel file, the second appellate court ruled "Appellant has now been given a fair trial and the jury found him guilty only of voluntary manslaughter with use of a firearm." People v. Sons, p. 103.

During the ALJ Hearing in 2000, and supported his innocence, "Two of the children who have been in his care in the past testified in this hearing, [redacted] and [redacted]. [redacted] described respondent (petitioner) as a grandfather figure, while [redacted] considers him like a father." (RJN, Exhibit C, p. 11 ¶25.) This evidence was all withheld from the court in this criminal case. See, People v. Stewart, 50 Cal.App.5th 755, 769-770:

> "The prosecution's constitutional duty to disclose all substantial material evidence favorable to an accused 'extends to evidence which may reflect on the credibility of a material witness. [Citation.] ... [S]uppression of substantial material evidence bearing on the credibility of a key prosecution witness is a denial of due process ...." [Citation.]' Thus, '[w]hen the "reliability of a given witness may well be determinative of guilt or innocence," nondisclosure of evidence affecting credibility' may require a new trial. (Giglio v. United States (1972) 405 U.S. 150, 154.)" (People v. Hayes (1992) 3 Cal.App.4th 1238, 1244-1245, fns. omitted.)."

The withheld evidence from the ALJ Hearing from 2000, was a reversible error with prejudice because the withheld evidence, for similar conduct the court concluded "The district court that dismissal with prejudice was appropriate because the government withheld key evidence favorable to the defense until after trial was underway-in clear violation of its duties under Brady-and dismissing without prejudice would allow the government to cure mistakes, to the detriment of the defendants." United States v. Bundy (9th Cir. 2020) 968 F.3d 1019, 1031. In petitioner's case the submitted false evidence, which Judge Bolton had ruled twice petitioner was not guilty of. See, United States v. Sedaghty (9th Cir. 2013) 738 F.3d 885, 898: ("FBI Special Agent contacted Cabral .... to pay her $7,500. Before trial, ... materials impeaching witnesses, and agent notes. The government, however, disclosed reports for only eight of the twenty interviews.); see also, Milke v. Ryan (9th Cir. 2010) 711 F.3d 998, 1007 ("Here, the state court's fact-finding process was defective in two ways. The first defect resulted from the prosecution's suppression of a suspension report in Saldate's personnel file. The report was clearly available to the state and it unquestionably constituted Brady and Giglio....)

The appellate court was without the evidence that Agent Housholder, was present at the ALJ Hearing, and working in privity with San Diego Detective Victoria Reden; which was a conspiracy to frame petitioner orchestrated by Housholder. See, Limone v. United States (Mass.Dist. 2003) 271 F.Supp.2d 345, 365:

> "As early as 1935, the Supreme Court expressly held "depriving a defendant of liberty through a deliberate deception of the court and jury by the presentation of testimony known to be perjured" violates the Constitution. Mooney v. Holohan, 294 U.S. 103, 112, 79 L.Ed. 791, 55 S.Ct. 340 (1935); see also Pyle v. Kansas, 317 U.S. 213, 216, 87 L.Ed. 214, 63 S.Ct. 177 (1946)."

The male prostitution of Raymond [redacted] was covered-up, and Judge Vallera Johnson's finding that he wasn't credible was not presented to the jury in violation of Brady v. Maryland, 373 U.S. 83, and this was crucial impeachment evidence. See, Amado v. Gonzalez (9th Cir.2013) 734 F.3d 936, 948-949:

> "Favorable evidence is not limited to evidence that is exculpatory, i.e., evidence that tends to prove the innocence of the defendant. Favorable evidence includes that which impeaches a prosecution witness. In Giglio v. United States, 405 U.S. 150, 154 .... (1972), "the Government's case depended almost entirely" on one witness, yet the prosecution failed to inform the defense that the witness testified in exchange for a promise from the government that he would not be prosecuted. . . . . The Supreme Court since has made clear that the prosecution must disclose all material impeachment evidence, not just evidence relating to cooperation agreements. See, Bagley, 473 U.S. at 676."

The Ninth Circuit further articulated, "A prosecutor's duty to reveal favorable, material information extends to information that is not in the possession of the individual prosecutor trying the case. In Kyles v. Whitley, 514 U.S. 419, 441-42...." Amado v. Gonzalez, 734 F.3d 936, p. 949.

Without this suppression of evidence that, FBI Agent Housholder working with the San Diego Detective Victorie Reden, privity was clear, and "The California Court of Appeal's Decision Was Contrary To Clearly Established Federal Law. A state court's "mistakes in reasoning or in predicate decisions" such as the wrong legal rule or framework "constitute error under the 'contrary to' prong of § 2254(d)(1)." Frantz v. Hazey, 533 F.3d 724, 734 (9th Cir.2008) (en banc); see Williams v. Taylor, 529 U.S. 362, 405-06, 120 S.Ct. 1495, 146 L.Ed.2d 389 (2000) (decision by a state court is "contrary to" Supreme Court's clearly established law if it "applies a rule that contradicts the governing law set forth in [Supreme Court's] cases"); see, e.g., id. (if, for example, "a state court were to reject a prisoner's claim of ineffective assistance of counsel on the grounds that the prisoner had not established by a preponderance of the evidence that the result of his criminal proceeding would have been different, that decision would be 'diametrically different,' 'opposite in character or nature,' and 'mutually opposed' to our clearly established precedent because we held in Strickland that the prisoner need only demonstrate a 'reasonable probability that ... the result of the proceeding would have been different'"); Frantz, 533 F.3d at 734...." Gardner v. Holland, 218 F.Supp.3d 1048, 1058-1059.

Like petitioner's case, "Ultimately, the trial court concluded that exclusion was proper under California Evidence Code section 352...." Gardner, ibid. p. 1058. The court herein used P.C. §352 to deny impeachment of Raymond [redacted]. See, People v. Rubino, 2008 Cal.App.Unpub.LEXIS 5883 **23-24.

The petitioner was denied the most fundamental right of confrontation of Iain [redacted], Raymond [redacted], and in effect Robert Housholder. See, Gardner v. Holland (N.D.Cal. 2016) 218 F.Supp.3d 1048, 1057

> "Under California law, "'the rule barring evidence of a victim's sexual conduct with persons other than the defendant does not 'make inadmissible any evidence offered to attack the credibility of the complaining witness as provided'" in California Evidence Code section 782. Cal.Ct.App. Opinion at 8 (quoting Cal. Evid.Code § 1103(c)(5)). Section 782(a)(4) requires the trial court to make two determinations. First, the trial court must determine that the evidence "regarding the sexual conduct of the complaining witness is relevant pursuant to [Evidence Code] Section 780," which pertains to witness credibility and allows consideration of a witness's "character for honesty or veracity of their opposites." Cal. Evid.Code § 780(e)."

The state courts used California Evidence Code section 352, as a reason to exclude evidence of Raymond [redacted] prior testimony from the ALJ Hearing, but it is unclear whether the record was provided; because the court of appeal erroneously ruled, "No Privity. Assuming arguendo the other four threshold requirements for application of collateral estoppel were satisfied, we conclude the threshold requirement of privity was not satisfied." People v. Rubino, 2008 Cal.App.Unpub. LEXIS 5883 *9.

The petitioner's situation clearly satisfied the definition of privity as defined by Merriam Websters Dictionary: "Privity".

> "Privity. 1a: a relationship between person who successively have a legal interest in the same right or property.
>
> b: an interest in a transaction, contract, or legal action to which one is not a party arising out of a relationship to one of the parties.
>
> 2: private or joint knowledge of a private matter; especially: cognizance implying concurrence."

The petitioner was deprived of confrontation of the alleged victims, Iain [redacted] and Timothy [redacted] by the prosecution's withholding impeachment evidence and the court's allowance of the suppression. See, Averilla v. Lopez (N.D.Cal.2012) 862 F. Supp.2d 987, 997-998:

> "The State Court Violated Petitioner's Confrontation Clause Rights by Improperly Limiting His Cross-Examination of the Prosecution's Two Leading Witnesses
>
> The confrontation Clause provides an accused the right to "be confronted with witnesses against him," and applies to the states through the Fourteenth Amendment, U.S. Const. amend. VI; Pointer v. Texas, 380 U.S. 400, 403, 85 S.Ct. 1065, 13 L.Ed.2d 923 (1965). The right of confrontation ensures that the reliability of evidence be "tested in the crucible of cross-examination." Crawford v. Washington, 541 U.S. 36, 61, 124 S.Ct. 1254, 158 L.Ed.2d 177 (2004)."

The petitioner was deprived of any type of confrontation of Robert Housholder, Raymond [redacted], Iain [redacted], and right to effective assistance of counsel. See, Frost v. Van Boening (9th Cir.2014) 757 F.3d 910, 914:

> "By preventing defense counsel from arguing reasonable doubt in closing, the trial judge "lessened the State's burden to some degree" and "infringed upon Frost's due process rights." Id. The trial court's "undue limitation on the scope of defense counsel's closing argument" also violated Frost's Sixth Amendment right to counsel under Herring, 422 U.S. at 862, which held that a defendant is entitled to closing argument. Frost, 161 P.3d at 365-66, 369."

The Agent Robert Housholder, and the FBI conspired to frame petitioner, for his past successful civil trial wherein ATF supported State Farm Insurance investigators; and for reporting Housholder for living with child molester Jim Echenroad. See, Limone v. United States (1st Cir.2009) 579 F.3d 79, 100.

The Supreme court has never suggested the doctrine of double jeopardy applies to the same proceeding. Indeed, it has consistently states it applies to "successive prosecutions." (Brown v. Ohio (1977) 432 U.S. 161, 167, fn. 6, and pp. 169-170.)

The Ninth Circuit ruled on double jeopardy under similar circumstances to petitioner in Wilkinson v. Gingrich (9th Cir. 2015) 806 F.3d 511, 513 ("The State brought the perjury prosecution after Wilkinson was acquitted of the speeding offense. We agree with the district court that the state appellate court unreasonably applied Ashe v. Swenson, 397 U.S. 436, 90 S.Ct. 1189, 25 L.Ed.2d 469 (1970), when it held that Wilkinson's acquittal in traffic court did not bar the subsequent perjury prosecution. See 28 U.S. § 2254(d)(1). The principle of collateral estoppel embodied in the Fifth Amendment's protection against double jeopardy, as clearly established in Ashe, precludes relitigation of ultimate issues that were necessarily decided in a prior proceeding between the parties. Ashe, 397 U.S. at 443.").

The petitioner was acquitted in the Administrative Law Court, by Judge Vallera J. Johnson, and the order was affirmed by the Director, Lawrence Bolton. Furthermore, Judge Lawrence Bolton, reiterated petitioner's acquittal for a scond time in the juvenile court proceedings to emancipate Paul Halmaghi. See, Ayala v. Dawson (1st Dist.2017) 13 Cal.App.5th 1319, 1326: ("Collateral estoppel "precludes relitigation of issues argued and decided in prior proceedings." (Lucido v. Superior Court (1990) 51 Cal.3d 335, 341 ....").

V

PETITIONER WAS SENTENCED TO LIFE IMPRISONMENT IN VIOLATION OF EX POST FACTO CLAUSE AND MILLER V. FLORIDA (1987) 483 U.S. 423; AND PEUGH V. UNITED STATES (2013) 569 U.S. 530

The petitioner is requesting that the Honorable Court will reconsider the January 10, 2024, order denying his ex post facto challenge for resentencing, because at 82 years old he was in dire need for relief from his unconstitutional conviction. See, People v. Hiscox (1st Dist.2006) 136 Cal.App.4th 253, 256:

> "We conclude it is the prosecution's responsibility to prove to the jury that the charged offenses occurred on or after the effective date of the stature providing for the defendant's punishment. When the evidence at trial does not establish that fact, the defendant is entitled to be sentenced under the formerly applicable statutes even if he raised no objection in the trial court."

The petitioner's "sentencing under 667.61 was prohibited by ex post facto principles. We remand for resentencing under the law in effect before the effective date of the statute." People v. Hiscox, 136 Cal.App.4th 253, 256.

Petitioner's offense at the time of allege crime required a sentence of three, six, or eight years, under Penal Code section 288(a). See also, Miller v. Florida (1987) 483 U.S. 423, and Lynch v. Superior Court (1995) 33 Cal.App.4th 1223.

The petitioner asserts that the offenses for which he was convicted did not fall within the sentence factors under Penal Code section 667.61, and he should have his sentence vacated. People v. Valenti (2016 243 Cal.App.4th 1140, 1174.

Petitioner should have been sentenced to three, six, or eight years, notwithstanding his innocence of these offenses.

CONCLUSION

For the foregoing reasons, petitioner's present confinement pursuant to his conviction in Case No. SCN167044 is illegal, and a writ of habeas corpus should issue.

Date: April 7, 2024.

Respectfully submitted,

Robert M. Rubino

Robert M. Rubino

IN THE SUPERIOR COURT OF CALIFORNIA

FOR THE COUNTY OF SAN DIEGO

FILED
Clerk of the Superior Court
NOV 16 2021
By: C. Balmaceda, Deputy

PEOPLE OF STATE OF CALIFORNIA, Plaintiff - Respondent, vs. ROBERT M. RUBINO, Defendant - Appellant.	Super. Court Case No. 167044 DEFENDANT'S POST-CONVICTION DISCOVERY APPLICATION PURSUANT TO PENAL CODE SECTION 1054.9

ROBERT M. RUBINO, #F-61501
R.J. DONOVAN CORRECTIONAL FACILITY
480 Alta Road, A3-101
San Diego, CA 92179

ROBERT M. RUBINO, No. F-61501
R.J.D. Correctional Facility
480 Alta Road, A-3-101
San Diego, CA 92179

SUPERIOR COURT OF CALIFORNIA

FOR COUNTY OF SAN DEIGO

PEOPLE OF STATE OF CALIFORNIA, Plaintiff, v. ROBERT M. RUBINO, Defendant.	Case No. SCN167044 DEFENDANT'S MOTION TO STRIKE PEOPLE'S AMENDED RESPONSE TO DEFENDANT'S REQUEST #15 PURSUANT TO PENAL CODE SECTION 1054.9(c)

TO THE SUPERIOR COURT OF THE STATE OF CALIFORNIA FOR THE COUNTY OF SAN DIEGO, HON. BRAD A. WEINREB, JUDGE:

Defendant moves to strike the People's Amended Response to Defendant's Request #15 as untimely filed; and pursuant to Penal Code § 1054.9(c), this was, "For purposes of this section "discovery materials" means material in the possession of the prosecution and law enforcement authorities to which the same defendant would have been entitled at time of trial."

Court's 03/21/22, Order for People's Response has not been

SUPERIOR COURT OF CALIFORNIA

FOR COUNTY OF SAN DIEGO

PEOPLE OF STATE OF CALIFORNIA, Plaintiff, v. ROBERT M. RUBINO, Defendant.	Case No. SCN167044 DEFENDANT'S REPLY TO PEOPLE'S OPPOSITION TO DEFENDANT'S APPLICATION PURSUANT TO PENAL CODE SECTION 1054.9

TO THE SUPERIOR COURT OF THE STATE OF CALIFORNIA FOR THE COUNTY OF SAN DIEGO, HONORABLE, BRAD WEINREB, JUDGE:

ROBERT M. RUBINO, No. F-61501
R.J. Donovan Correctional Fac.
480 Alta Road, A-3-101
San Diego, CA 91279

ROBERT M. RUBINO, No. F-61501
R.J. Donovan Correctional Facility
480 Alta Road, A-3 #149
San Diego, CA 92179

ROBERT BONTA, ATTORNEY GENERAL OF CALIFORNIA
SUMMER STEPHAN, DISTRICT ATTORNEY OF SAN DIEGO COUNTY
455 Golden Gate ave., Suite 11000
San Francisco, CA 94102-7004

November 03, 2024

[Re: People v. Robert M. Rubino, SCN167044.]

Dear, Robert Bonta:

On October 08, 2024, a Petition for writ of habeas corpus was filed in the Court of Appeal Fourth Appellate District, Division One, Case No. D084961.

Detective Victoria Reden, who brought these false charges against me; testified that she got a black light out of my room (I was over 60 yrs. old, and did not own one). The black light was in my Granddaughter's room to light up a black light poster. At trial T.J. [redacted] said there was no black light in my room.

Reden wanted the black light to find body fluids to plant on T.J.'s boxers. Also, I suffered from urine discharge on clothes, especially my boxers.

Since Det. Reden claimed I had this black light in my room for some purpose. To prove this, why did she not fingerprint the black light? It was ceramic with a glass light which must have fingerprints on it. EVEN NOW. If the D.A. or A.G. cares about the truth that Reden tricked the D.A. into believing my guilt, why not get the black light out of evidence and fingerprint it? It will not have my fingerprints on it!!

Reden used the black light to find and move (plant) bodily fluids to T.J.'s boxers, 5 sperm and DNA of an unknown male. Further, Reden told the lab tech who testified, where to look to find a spot on T.J.'s boxers. How did Reden know the location if she did not plant this microscopic evidence?

Reden took my comforter off my bed; but I was using this from the boys room for friend to use when they slept over after the dog chewed up my King size comforter.

Iain [redacted] and T.J. [redacted] stole money from my wallet; and stole two game boys which they fought over and came up missing. Some $260 games.

These are further motives to lie for Housholder and Reden when in fear of these crimes also. Iain [redacted] downloaded the semi-nude photo and was witnessed showing it to T.J. by Cheyenne [redacted], supporting my innocence.

I, declare under the penalty of perjury the foregoing is true and correct, executed on November 03, 2024.

Robert M. Rubino

Robert M. Rubino

SUPERIOR COURT OF CALIFORNIA

County of San Diego

DATE: January 10, 2024 **DEPT. 5** **REPORTER A: Janet Giannantonio** **CSR# 12717**

PRESENT HON. **Brad A. Weinreb** **REPORTER B:** **CSR# 0**

JUDGE **TAPE NUMBER(S):**

CLERK: Susan Marie Smith

BAILIFF: Rudy Gertzki **REPORTER'S ADDRESS: P.0 BOX 128**

SAN DIEGO, CA 92112-4104

SCN167044 **THE PEOPLE OF THE STATE OF CALIFORNIA, Plaintiff**
By: Kimberly Roth

vs.

OAM677 **ROBERT M. RUBINO, Defendant**

By: Emily Rose-Weber

The matter is before the Court for a Status Conference regarding- PC1054.9 - Court issues the following Order- All discovery and/or Brady issues raised by defendant Rubino are deemed moot and no further hearings will be set. The court further denies defendant Rubino's request to appear for a status hearing in order to address a separate invalid sentence allegation.

Defendant Rubino repeatedly ignored the Court's directive to not correspond with the Court while represented by counsel and that that the Court would neither receive nor respond to such correspondences. Despite that, in a February 2023 filing that discussed *his discovery related issues, defendant Rubino alleged he also suffers from an invalid sentence. He did so in a perfunctory and* conclusory manner and without legal analysis. It is forfeited and waived and need not be addressed. (*People v. Harper* (2000) 82 Cal.App.4th 1413, 1419, fn. 4, 98 Cal.Rptr.2d 894.) Assuming the court treats the allegation as a new habeas claim, it is also denied for the same reasons and otherwise untimely and successive. In re Marquez (2007) 153 Cal.App.4th 1, 13; In re Clark (1993) 5 Cal.4th 750.) No order to show cause as to that allegation will issue.

January 10, 2024

Hon. Brad A. Weinreb

By U.S. Constitutional law every defendant has the absolute right to communicate anytime with his judge whether or not he has a lawyer, because corrupt Weinreb, like all judges, has absolute immunity from prosecution, just to shut me up, he makes this unlawful Court order as his participation in the "secret judicial code of silence", judges use to protect each other and their co-conspirators and to conceal their violations and crime against defendants like me.

With impunity he violates my 1st, 6th and 14th Amendment U.S. Constitutional rights and there is nothing I can do about this except pray I can get away from Weinreb and Maino into the federal Court where the U.S. Constitution is followed and respected.

I declare under the penalty of perjury the above is true and correct.

Dated: July 4, 2024.

In God's Hands, I am.

Robert M. Rubino

Trial Minute Order Template/5-02

Appendix C: Continued Report on Medical Condition and Intent to Sue

I have and continue to fully document my ongoing open leg infection of unknown type which I caught in RJD-AD Seg's filthy conditions. The CDCR has a history of wanton and callous incompetent and grossly negligent inmate medical care. When the federal court, in response to overwhelming evidence of CDCR's substantial and often grossly negligent medical care of prisoners, appointed a Court Monitor to oversee and report to the Court to see that the improvements the Court mandated were being implemented. The singular motivation of the CDCR was to end this monitoring process as soon as possible and be rid of the monitor. The CDCR's initial request to remove the monitor was strongly denied by the Court because the improvements claimed by the CDCR were greatly inadequate. Given that, in the J & J powder cancer case, the jury awarded 300 million dollars (5% of J & J's annual profit) to prevent further corruption and to change policies, I believe that, in my case, in which there are four additional incidents of CDCR's medical incompetence on top of the current leg wound infection horror, such an award is potentially available for me as well.

1) In college, I was in a terrible auto accident in which I ripped all my back muscles from the base of my skull to the base of my spine as my car was forced down a 60 foot embankment. Both of my kidneys were damaged and, years later, when a strong antibiotic was discovered, my chronic kidney infections could finally be addressed and controlled. Because of this experience, I am intimately familiar with the symptoms of an oncoming kidney infection. I experienced such symptoms here at RJD and made numerous medical requests for help, all of which were flatly ignored: I was repeatedly told to go to my cell and rest. I was later found unconscious on the floor of the mess hall at dinner. I later woke up in Bakersfield, CA's Mercy Hospital in its ICU on dialysis. The attending doctor was furious: I had almost died from a kidney infection that could easily have been diagnosed with a simple in-office urine test. My doctor called the medical care at RJD "incompetent." I was in the ICU with on and off dialysis for a week. When I returned to RJD after Mercy Hospital had saved my life, I was so weak that it took almost three months for me to fully recover. Even the CO's recognized that I was too weak to stand and allowed me to sit on my bunk during the 4 PM count, in which, at the time, inmates were required to stand up. I was also not able

to shower or bathe on my own for the first 4-5 weeks after I returned, and Medical had to assign an inmate healthcare worker to me to assist me during that time.

2) One day, at about 5 PM, Dr. Silva MD, my primary physician, called me to the plaza gate and said, "I'm not going to let them kill you. I have an ambulance waiting to take you to Alvarado Hospital." The date of each medical incident can be found in my hospital records. At Alvarado, Dr. Butcher MD told me that I had a gallbladder infection. He would have to remove my gallbladder arthroscopically with three small incisions. When I recovered from anesthesia, I did have the three small incisions, but I also had a large incision on my side which required 15 staples to close. Dr. Butcher was clearly angry and stated that, because of the "greatly negligent care" provided to me by RJD, I had almost died. The prison MD had, for *weeks*, misdiagnosed my gallbladder infection. Because of the resulting delay in treatment, my gallbladder had disintegrated and was covering all adjacent organs. If he had tried to remove the gallbladder from these organs, he would have damaged these adjacent organs, which would have killed me. He had inserted a drain in my side, requiring the large incision to do so, and was giving me powerful antibiotics to attempt to kill the infection. He told me that, if this infection returned in the future and began to resist the antibiotics, he would have to operate to surgically remove the remaining gallbladder but that I would only have a 5-10% chance of surviving such an operation. I was once again put into the ICU.

3) On a different occasion, I had complained several times to medical that I had a fever and felt cold chest tightness and was repeatedly told that "it [was] just a cold" and to "go back to [my] cell and rest... and drink plenty of water." On my third visit to the prison's medical clinic, I was dismissed once again, given only cough drops to alleviate my symptoms. The following day, I was found at late afternoon count semiconscious on the floor of my cell! I was rushed via ambulance to Scripps Trauma ER. The MD was furious and shocked, as I would later learn. He told me that I had pneumonia and would not survive until morning! I was receiving massive doses of antibiotics through an IV for over six hours—these drugs were so strong that I was struggling not to vomit. Once I was stabilized, I was taken by ambulance to Alvarado Hospital and was placed in **Isolation ICU** for twelve days! Everyone who entered my room had to wear a mask, including the CO's who were stationed outside my cell. Twelve days later, when hospital tests showed that I had cleared the infection, I still could not be released until the San Diego Health Department had had a chance to test me and approve my release.

My pneumonia was clearly yet another result of grossly negligent and incompetent medical care. It was obvious that the medical care provided by CDCR was still well below the standard of care that the federal court had ordered that inmates should receive, and that the court's monitoring of CDCR must continue.

4) Up to this point, I have only detailed medical incidents which occurred as a result of the depraved indifference and gross negligence of the CDCR medical staff. I must also speak on the ways in which CDCR has purposefully done medical harm to me. Firstly, it is a verified fact in my medical history that the type of food served in prison, which is often greasy or spicy, gives me chronic diarrhea. I filed a lawsuit in 2013 to address this problem (the ruling of which is publicly available), and the court ordered that I was to receive either a proper diet based on my medical information or $180 per month to buy food from the canteen. This order was appealed and vacated by CDCR sub rosa, and it was ordered that I receive not just the one quarterly package allowed to inmates but also two more packages each quarter in other inmates' names from my family. I paid inmates $25 to get these packages.

On or about 11/8/2020, Dr. Wilkerson MD, Chief of Oncology at Alvarado Hospital, informed me via telemed call that I have chronic lymphocytic leukemia (CLL). Of all forms of leukemia, this was the one "non-lethal" form; I could live a very long life, but I could not donate blood or organs. He also warned me that my CLL, along with my type II diabetes, congestive heart failure, weak heart function, and my leg swelling had weakened my immune system, and that, if I caught COVID-19, it would likely end my life. At this point, no vaccine had yet been developed for the coronavirus. My primary physician echoed this warning to me that same morning. I received a COVID-19 test and tested negative.

About two hours later, I was called to the Program Office by two sergeants. At this point I was working on publishing a book exposing the crimes and cover-ups committed by the FBI. I had published two other books in the past with similar content, and CDCR was aware of this.

One of the CO sergeants said to me, "Why the f__k are you writing another f__king book? Don't you know who you're f__king with?" I replied that, although I was in prison, I still had my First Amendment rights and that I intended to exercise this right and publish my book.

About two hours after this confrontation, two CO's came to my cell and told me to "roll it up." I was going to the gym quarantine for COVID-19. I told them that this had to be a mistake—I had tested negative for the coronavirus earlier that very day. This obvious issue was summarily ignored.

When I refused to go with the officers, they handcuffed me in my wheelchair and forced me to go with them, removing the handcuffs only when we reached the Plaza Gate. Prison regulations state that, since I refused to comply with the order to "roll it up," I should have received a disciplinary 115. However, I did not receive a 115; CDCR did not want a 115 on the record because, if I died of COVID-19 in the gym quarantine, such a record would prove that I had been intentionally murdered. These CO's wanted me to contract the coronavirus and die in the gym with other sick and dying inmates. Furthermore, to increase the chances that I would contract COVID-19 and die, the CO's did not transport my just received $220.xx Walkenhorst package of food in order to force me to eat only state food and thus weaken my immune system further by redeveloping my chronic diarrhea.

Over the next two weeks, I spent time with David D., who had a COVID-19 infection that progressed and eventually took his life. I am blessed to have spent time with David in his last days. Father God, unto Your Hands we commend Brother David's soul for eternity with You!

The diarrhea came with a vengeance. For two-and-a-half weeks, I endured awful diarrhea before, exhausted, I began a hunger strike, only consuming coffee and water. This hunger strike lasted 15 days and I lost 13 pounds. During this time, a concerned party was advocating for me, contacting the California governor's office and the local FBI. Five weeks later, Ms. Sara Smith, the Chief Ombudsman for all California, and Sgt Hampton came to speak with me. I was told that, if I stopped my hunger strike, they would bring me my missing (stolen) food package. However, about a week passed without my package being returned to me.

On January 1, 2022, I was released from quarantine. It is a statement of fact that everyone apart from me who were made to quarantine spent **only two weeks** in quarantine before being released. I was the **only one who quarantined in the gym for seven weeks!** There was no valid reason, medical or otherwise, to keep me in quarantine for that long; it is evident that I was only kept this long because I was meant to contract COVID-19 and die.

I did become COVID-19 positive upon release and was sent upon release to be evaluated by my primary care physician, Dr. Sedighi. He told me that he could not medically explain how I was able to survive seven weeks in quarantine with COVID-19 and how I had been completely asymptomatic. In addition, my type II diabetes had disappeared. My A1C was 5.5.

A few months later, my cardiologist, Dr. Hernandez, told me after an angiogram to check my triple bypass graph that the bypass must have been performed recently because my charts were perfect. When I told Dr. Hernandez that my bypass was done 30 years ago, he could not believe it. He had no explanation for how my charts were perfect, but I did: God did this for me just as He saved my life when Slay tried to kill me. Thank You Father God!

By the way, inmate Slay inflicted multiple stab wounds around my right eye and cheek. Initially, the CO's thought that I had completely lost that eye, but the 60+ stitches it took to close my multiple infected cheek and eye wounds left no scar at all and my eye was left intact! Another miracle from God which the MD's had no explanation for. Do you believe God would heal, save, and protect me so many times if I were guilty?

I declare under the penalty of perjury the above is true and correct.

Dated: 2/26/2024

In God's Hands, I am,
Robert M. Rubino

P.S. I will sue the DOJ, CDCR, and San Diego County to force each to stop their corrupt practices. I will settle each lawsuit for **only one dollar** ***if*** they guarantee that they will stop their corruption, or I will ask each jury to award me 5% of each of their annual budgets, like the Johnson and Johnson Baby Powder lawsuit awarded, to force change **to protect my fellow Americans!** RMR.

Appendix D: Testimony About Medical Miracles

Brothers and Sisters, Do You Believe in Miracles from God?

God has blessed me with a number of unexplained physical medical miracles which cannot be explained by modern medicine. He would not have blessed me with these miracles if I was not completely innocent of my false convictions in His knowing eyes. We now have proof of my innocence, but, of course, I must go through all the judicial barriers to freedom. I will give CBS-TV News exclusive full authority to investigate and obtain all my CDCR and hospital medical and legal records to verify the existence of these medical miracles provided that CBS will share its findings of these miracles with all other news media, both on TV and in print.

1) Brief relevant medical history. My DOB - 6/25/41 - at age 50 I had a massive heart attack and triple bypass - I lost ⅓ of heart function - congestive heart failure, CHF - heart only effectively pumps at 29% and not 85% normal heart function.
2) Age 60 - 2007 - I had type II diabetes, CHF, lymphocytic leukemia, spinal and other arthritic problems - I refused spinal arthritic removal surgery and was told my spine would become very painful and cripple me. Alvarado Hospital Chief of Oncology, Dr. Wilkerson MD, asked CDCR to grant me compassionate release because the new COVID-19 infection could kill me with my weak and compromised immune system. At that time, I was COVID-19 negative, and no vaccine had yet been discovered. I was wrongly placed in the gym quarantine where COVID-19 infected and dying inmates were usually kept for two weeks. I became COVID-19 infected and was held for seven weeks to kill me and to prevent my exposing an FBI agent who is a child molester. I lost 14 pounds in the gym. Dr, Shinghi MD, upon my release, could not medically explain how I survived my COVID-19 infection asymptomatically. Even more medically unexplainably, my type II diabetes was cured, and my AIC was only 5.5—which it still is now! Cured!
3) 10/7/22 - I was repeatedly stabbed in my right eye and right cheek as inmate Slay attempted to murder me (he was convicted of my attempted murder). My right eye was gouged out and destroyed and, along with my right cheek, required over 60 stitches to

close the wounds. Inmates present in the dayroom thought I had died. God has completely restored my right eye with full vision. I have no facial or right cheek scars from the wounds and from the 60+ stitches I received in the ER. Inmate Slay had shouted that he wanted to kill me, and I should have died or at least have become blind in my right eye. For two months, Internal Affairs placed me in the "hole" with nothing where I lost 18 lbs. while they investigated. I was the victim! Remember, gouged out eyes do not regenerate to normal as my eye did completely. There is no modern medical explanation for my complete facial and visual restoration except that these are miracles granted to me by the love and grace of God!

4) 3/1/25 - By the way, for the past 33 years I have had congestive heart failure, I have had to wear compression leg stockings and take 2 mg of a diuretic in the AM and take 1 mg more in the PM to void the excessive fluid in my legs. These meds are only 75% effective to void my leg fluid retention. Excess leg fluid can build up into my chest, press against my heart, and cause immediate heart failure and death. The heart does not heal, and, after my massive heart attack years ago, ⅓ of my heart has not functioned. My heart has pumped only at 29% and not at the normal heart rate of 85+%. Now, a new EKG has proven that my heart now suddenly pumps not at 29% but at 49% effectiveness, and my leg fluid has become much reduced. There is no medical explanation for the increased heart function. Instead of 2 mg AM diuretic and 1 mg PM diuretic to reduce leg fluid by only 75%, now, with no compression stockings worn, and only 1 mg PM diuretic on average, I have 90% of leg fluid gone! God has blessed me with this miraculous medical heart healing! Hearts do not heal as mine has!

5) 10/3/23 - Had left knee surgically replaced at Alvarado Hospital. I got a "water blister," which was an open leg wound the size of a silver dollar from the excessive IV fluid retention after surgery and my 29% heart pumping ability. This wound became infected with an unknown infection while in RJD prison. I was sent to the Centinela Prison Hospital Unit for two months with a 23 hour per day lockdown and 24 hour care. Four MD wound care specialists could not identify or cure this open leg wound infection with many antibiotics. Fed up with this 23 hour lockdown and having nothing but an empty cell and no personal property of mine, I left. They said my leaving and refusing medical care could kill me or make me lose my leg. I returned to RJD prison, and, after one more month of useless antibiotics, I refused all treatment of this open leg wound and left my life in God's hands. Two weeks later, my open leg

wound healed completely, and the infection was cured by God. Also medically unexplained is how this awful unidentified leg wound infection never infected the open knee surgical incision wound only three inches above this water blister. This infection was in my blood. The MDs expected me to need the replaced knee removed until this infection was cured or the leg amputated. God did not allow this infected water blister to infect my just-replaced knee. Because I trusted in Him, He cured my infection and water blister open wound. Believe!!

6) About five years ago, MDs wanted to operate on my spine to remove the arthritis which was beginning to painfully cripple me. I refused and was warned that this spinal arthritis would become more painful and cripple me and my ability to walk. On 3/22/25 - 10:30 AM, I went into a comatose deep sleep for three hours, unlike any sleep I can remember. Upon waking, unlike my usual awful wakeup AM back spinal pain, I had ZERO spinal back arthritic pain - NONE! Also, now suddenly I could freely get up and walk about and could even do a half squat down and other physical knee movements - no pain! For several years I could only walk a few steps holding on to something. In shock, I said nothing. For the past four months, I've had extensive medical tests to approve my upcoming right knee replacement. Now I live in an ADA wheelchair accessible cell. Riverside University Hospital has approved my right knee replacement. On 3/27/25, I decided to try to walk from the back of the chow hall to my cell, and so, for the next week, holding onto my wheelchair, I slowly walked the 800+ steps to my cell! My spinal weakness is gone! God has cured my spine! Also, I have no leg muscle pain from suddenly walking after years of wheelchair dependency. God has again blessed me with a miracle.
7) I do not include the three times I barely survived the grossly negligent medical care I received in CDCR. Perhaps I should include these as miracles as well. (A) CDCR misdiagnosed a kidney infection. I was found unconscious on the chow hall floor and was placed in the ICU at Bakersfield Hospital on dialysis for a week. I actually felt Jesus carry me out of an indescribable blackness - void into the light. It was a religious exalted presence with Jesus I cannot fully explain to you. It did take me two months to recover. The hospital MD said he was surprised I survived and was furious that my kidney infection was not properly diagnosed by CDCR. He said any second year medical student could have tested my urine and found this infection. (B) One night, the prison MD actually said, "I'm not going to let them kill you. I have an ambulance waiting to

take you to the hospital. You must have your gallbladder removed." At Alvarado Hospital, Dr. Butcher MD (which is his real name, and he is a great doctor) told me that it would only take three small incisions to remove my diseased gallbladder. When I returned from surgery the following day, I had the three incisions plus another incision which required 15 staples to close. My gallbladder, not having been examined for an extended period of time, had deteriorated over all my adjoining organs. If they tried to remove the gallbladder, it would damage the other organs, and I had only a 10% chance to survive. They put in a drain and gave me massive amounts of antibiotics. If it returned in the future, the diseased gallbladder could hopefully be treated with antibiotics, but, again, I had only a 10% chance to survive the removal of the diseased gallbladder. Dr. Butcher MD could not believe that the CDCR MDs did not discover such an easily diagnosed diseased gallbladder. (C) I was rushed to Scripps Trauma ER in a semi-conscious state with pneumonia. The ER doctor said I would not have lived until morning, and he could not believe that the CDCR MDs did not diagnose such an advanced case of pneumonia. For over six hours, I was treated with massive doses of antibiotics then transferred by ambulance to Alvarado Hospital and placed in its intensive isolated ICU for 11 days. I could not be released from the Alvarado ICU until the San Diego Health Department had cleared me of this viral pneumonia. I've had pneumonia five times while incarcerated.

Praise God! Believe! Woe to those who have eyes and do not see, ears that hear and do not hear, and hearts that are hardened, too. God would not do these miracles and save me if I was not innocent in His all-knowing eyes!

I share these miracles with you so that you may believe in and experience the power and love of God. I am 84 years old and will not meet my God with vengeance, hate, or anger in my heart for those who have falsely and maliciously convicted and imprisoned me these past 21+ years. Without any mental reservation, I forgive them all, and I pray they seek God's forgiveness and save their souls from damnation. So many judges and prosecutors violate God's commandment, "Thou shall not bear false witness," as they falsely or unjustly prosecute many like me. God does not promise us justice in this world but only to console us if we let Him. I am at total peace and I pray you will also find God's solace and peace and never give up on your personal struggle.

RJD - B9-130
480 Alta Road
San Diego, CA 92179

In God's Hands, I Am
Robert M. Rubino, F61501

I declare under the penalty of perjury that the foregoing is true and correct.

Dated: 4/12/2025 Robert M. Rubino

June 25, 2024, I filed a petition for writ of mandate and a motion for judicial notice consolidated in the Court of Appeal 4th Appellate District, Case No. D084329. On July 9, 2024, the Court of Appeal granted judicial notice of my innocence. November 12, 2024, the Court of Appeal in a petition for writ of habeas corpus unjustly refused to consider the suppressed evidence made part of record by other Court justices on above case in new case No's D084524; and D084961.

RMR

COURT OF APPEAL, FOURTH APPELLATE DISTRICT

DIVISION ONE

STATE OF CALIFORNIA

ROBERT M. RUBINO, Petitioner, v. THE SUPERIOR COURT OF SAN DIEGO COUNTY, Respondent; THE PEOPLE, Real Party in Interest.	D084329 (San Diego County Super. Ct. No. SCN167044)

THE COURT:

The petition for writ of mandate and request for judicial notice have been read and considered by Presiding Justice McConnell and Associate Justices O'Rourke and Rubin. The request for judicial notice is granted except as to Exhibit D, which pertains to the title page of Petitioner's book. (See Evid. Code, § 452 [setting forth requirements for judicial notice].) The petition is denied.

McCONNELL, P. J.

Copies to: All parties

ROBERT M. RUBINO, No. F-61501
R.J. Donovan Correctional Facility
450 Alta Road, B-9 #130
San Diego, CA 92179

April 12, 2025

CBS / Georgetown University

I am a Catholic and a graduate of Georgetown University '65. I will give full authority to CBS and to G.U. Law School to have full access to all my legal records and files, and I will give full authority to CBS and to G.U. Medical School to examine all my extensive California Dept. of Corrections medical files and all my hospital records to verify these enclosed miracles if either Mother Church or CBS is interested in these miracles or in my innocence.

In God's Hands, I Am
Robert M. Rubino